Favorite **BiBLe** Children

GRADES 3&4

Rainbow Books

Rainbow Publishers • P.O. Box 261129 • San Diego, CA 92196

Favorite Bible Children

GRADES 3&4

Linda Washington

To my brothers, Chris and Stan, and my sisters-in-law,
Lisa and Gia, all of whom are some of God's favorite children.

FAVORITE BIBLE CHILDREN FOR GRADES 3&4
©1999 by Rainbow Publishers
ISBN 1-885358-78-4
Rainbow reorder #RB36914

Rainbow Publishers
P.O. Box 261129
San Diego, CA 92196

Illustrator: Chuck Galey
Cover Illustrator: Helen Lannis
Editor: Christy Allen

Scriptures are from the Holy Bible: New International Version (North American Edition), ©1973, 1978, 1984 by the International Bible Society. Used by permission of Zondervan Bible Publishers.

Printed in the United States of America

Table of Contents

Memory Verse Index 7
Introduction 9
Note to Parents 11

Isaac (Genesis 12-22)
Isaac Is Born 13
Abraham's Test 14
The Promise Explained 16
The Promise Is Given 18

Ishmael (Genesis 21:8-21)
God Hears Ishmael 19

Jacob and Esau (Genesis 25:19-34)
Keep the Peace! 22

Joseph (Genesis 37)
A Colorful Coat 24
The Favorite Son 26

Miriam (Exodus 2:1-10)
Baby in the Water 28
Our Helper 30

Samuel (1 Samuel 1-3)
God Calls Samuel 31
Hannah Asks for a Son 33

David (1 Samuel 16-18)
David Fights Goliath 34
David Is Anointed King 36
Pals for Life 38

The Widow of Zarephath's Son (1 Kings 17:7-24)
Back from the Dead 39
Saving a Widow's Son 40

The Widow's Sons (2 Kings 4:1-7)
Elisha Helps the Widow 41
Helping the Helpless 42

The Shunammite's Son (2 Kings 4:8-37)
Kindness from Strangers 43
Trusted to Help 45

Naaman's Servant Girl (2 Kings 5:1-16)
Serving the Master 46
A Difficult Kindness 47

Joash (2 Kings 11)
Road to the Throne 49

Josiah (2 Kings 22:1-11, 18-20)
Doing Right for God 51

Joash and Josiah (2 Kings 11; 22:1-11, 18-20)
Setting an Example 52

Naming Babies (Isaiah 7:14; 8:1-10; 9:6-7)
Bible-Times Names 53
Names of Jesus 55

John the Baptist (Luke 1:5-25, 57-80)
The Gift of a Son 56
John's Special Vow 58
John's Arrival 60

Jesus (Genesis 3:1-7, 15; Matthew 2; Luke 1-2)
Mary Is Chosen 61
A Savior Is Born 62
Jesus Is Here! 63
Gifts for a King 65
Escape to Egypt 67
What's in a Name 68
A Good Son 69
One Amazing Life 73
A Son to Come 75

The Boy Who Gave His Lunch (John 6:1-13)
Lunch for 5,000 77
Bread to Eat 79

Jairus' Daughter (Matthew 9:18-19, 23-25)
Through the Crowd 81
An Impossible Task 82
Healing a Daughter 84
Help for the Hard Times 86

Blessing the Children (Matthew 19:13-15)
Coming to Jesus 89
Jesus Welcomes the Children 91
All Are Welcome 92

Answer Key 95

Memory Verse Index

Old Testament

Genesis 18:14 The Promise Explained..........16

1 Samuel 16:7 David Is Anointed King 36

Psalm 9:10 Kindness from Strangers........43

Trusted to Help 45

Psalm 23:4 Escape to Egypt 67

Psalm 25:9 Doing Right for God.............51

Psalm 29:2 Gifts for a King....................65

Psalm 46:1 Road to the Throne 49

Psalm 46:10 Baby in the Water 28

Our Helper 30

Psalm 127:3 The Promise Is Given 18

Psalm 145:13 Isaac Is Born 13

Psalm 146:9 Elisha Helps the Widow 41

Helping the Helpless.............42

Proverbs 17:17 Pals for Life 38

Proverbs 22:1 What's in a Name 68

Isaiah 9:6 Bible-times Names 53

Names of Jesus 55

Isaiah 49:13 God Hears Ishmael 19

Zechariah 4:6 David Fights Goliath.............34

New Testament

Matthew 6:25 Bread to Eat 79

Matthew 6:25-26 Saving a Widow's Son 40

Matthew 19:14 Coming to Jesus................89

Jesus Welcomes the Children..91

All Are Welcome 92

Mark 9:23 Through the Crowd 81

An Impossible Task 82

Healing a Daughter 84

Luke 1:37 Mary Is Chosen 61

Luke 2:11 A Savior Is Born 62

Jesus Is Here!...................63

Luke 6:35 Serving the Master...........46

A Difficult Kindness 47

Luke 6:38 Lunch for 5,000 77

Luke 10:21 God Calls Samuel 31

Luke 11:9 Hannah Asks for a Son 33

John 10:10 One Amazing Life 73

Acts 6:3-4 John's Special Vow 58

Acts 10:34-25 A Colorful Coat 24

The Favorite Son 26

Romans 6:23 A Son to Come 75

Romans 12:18 Keep the Peace! 22

2 Corinthians 9:15 The Gift of a Son.............56

Ephesians 6:1 A Good Son 69

1 Timothy 4:12 Setting an Example 52

Hebrews 11:6 Back from the Dead.........39

Hebrews 13:6 Help for the Hard Times ..86

James 1:12 Abraham's Test.................14

Introduction

No one is too young to begin learning about God and His great power and love. Not only can young children learn, they can be an example for other believers. Paul says in 1 Timothy 4:12: "Don't let anyone look down on you because you are young, but set an example for the believers in speech, in life, in love, in faith and in purity." God sees our hearts, not our ages.

Throughout the Bible there are numerous examples of children and young people making a difference. The Lord Himself chose to come to earth as a baby. What better way to teach young children about God than to use other children as examples! The crafts, games, puzzles and activities in *Favorite Bible Children* are designed to let children know that they can be instruments of God.

Each activity includes:

√ **Bible child's name or identifier**
√ **lesson title:** highlighting a Bible story
√ **Scripture reference:** for Bible story
√ **memory verse:** to reinforce the story, lesson or activity
√ **What You Need:** a materials list for the lesson
√ **What to Do:** how to conduct the activity
√ **What to Say:** a short lesson

The memory verse index on page 7 will help you match lessons to other Bible-teaching tools or curriculum you are using. To help keep activity costs to a minimum, send home the reproducible Note to Parents on page 11 to request help in gathering supplies. And remember: all patterns may be duplicated. You only need to buy one book for your entire class!

These crafts and activities focus on just a few of the children whose stories are recorded in the Bible. It was because these children were willing to be used by God and were obedient to Him that God was able to do great things through them. Whether their actions facilitated a miracle such as the little boy sharing his lunch with Jesus or the encouragement of others as with Timothy, God was able to use them because they loved and honored Him. Your very young children are just starting to learn about God. Use *Favorite Bible Children* to teach them that no matter how young they are, God can use them.

To Families of Third and Fourth Graders

We have some exciting activities planned for use in teaching Bible lessons this year. Some of these crafts and projects use ordinary household items. We'd like to ask your help in saving these items for our activities:

❑	acrylic paint	❑	fishing line
❑	bandannas	❑	marbles
❑	9" x 13" baking pans	❑	men's old shirts
❑	buckets	❑	sandbox shovels
❑	dowel rods	❑	spoons
❑	fabric glue	❑	string
❑	felt		

Please bring the items on _____

Thank you for your help!

To Families of Third and Fourth Graders

We have some exciting activities planned for use in teaching Bible lessons this year. Some of these crafts and projects use ordinary household items. We'd like to ask your help in saving these items for our activities:

❑	acrylic paint	❑	fishing line
❑	bandannas	❑	marbles
❑	9" x 13" baking pans	❑	men's old shirts
❑	buckets	❑	sandbox shovels
❑	dowel rods	❑	spoons
❑	fabric glue	❑	string
❑	felt		

Please bring the items on _____

Thank you for your help!

Isaac

Isaac Is Born
Genesis 21:1-18

Memory Verse

The Lord is faithful to all his promises and loving toward all he has made.
~Psalm 145:13

What You Need

• white construction paper
• pens
• acrylic paint
• water
• shallow bowls
• 9" x 13" baking pans
• spoons
• two marbles
• clear self-stick plastic
• men's old shirts

What to Do

Print the memory verse on the chalkboard for the children to copy. Give each child one-third of a piece of white construction paper. Have the children print the memory verse on the construction paper. Pour paint into separate shallow dishes and drop two marbles into each dish. Split the students into groups of three. Show how to "marblize" a memory verse by taping one of the memory verse papers in the bottom of a pan, then use a spoon to place the marbles onto the paper. Tip the pan to allow the marble to roll around. Allow the children to use as many colors as they like. Designate a certain amount of time for each memory verse if the children are working in groups. Help them apply clear self-stick plastic to their finished and dried creations so they can use them as book marks.

What to Say

God did what He said He would do: Abraham and Sarah finally had the son God promised them! Abraham was 100 years old at the time. Sarah was 90. Abraham and Sarah named the baby Isaac. This special birth is an example of how we can know that God keeps His promises. Can you think of some promises God kept in your life? Let the students respond. You can use this bookmark as a reminder that God is faithful.

Isaac

Abraham's Test
℘ Genesis 22:1-19 ℘

Memory Verse

Blessed is the man who perseveres under trial, because when he has stood the test, he will receive the crown of life that God has promised to those who love him.

~James 1:12

What You Need

• page 15

What to Do

Photocopy page 15 for each child. Let the children choose parts to act out the play. Have the children move around the room as if journeying to Moriah. After the children act out the play script, "debrief" by explaining that God never intended for Abraham to sacrifice his son. God just wanted to see whether Abraham loved God more than his own flesh and blood.

What to Say

Quick! Think of the hardest test you've ever faced. You may think the hardest test was the math or spelling quiz you had in school. Abraham was given a harder test, one that many of us might have failed. The test involved his son, the promised son for whom Abraham and Sarah had waited for so long. We'll face many tests and problems. But God always provides the strength and courage to meet the challenges. Why do you think Abraham named the mountain "The-Lord-Will-Provide"?

On Mount Moriah

Characters

• **voice of God**

• **Abraham**

• **narrator**

• **Isaac**

• **two extras**

Narrator: Abraham loved God and obeyed Him. But one day, God told Abraham to do something unusual.

Voice of God: Abraham!

Abraham: Here I am.

Voice of God: Take your son, your only son whom you love, and offer him as a sacrifice in the land of Moriah.

Narrator: Abraham was very sad. But he wanted to obey God. So he got up early and took Isaac to the land of Moriah. He took two other men with them, plus wood for the burnt offering. On the third day of their journey, Abraham saw the place where he had to go.

Abraham: Stay here. My son and I will go over to that place and worship God. Then we will come back.

Narrator: Abraham gave the wood to Isaac, while he took a torch and a knife.

Isaac: We have wood and fire. But where is the lamb for the sacrifice?

Abraham: God Himself will provide it, my son.

Narrator: But when they arrived at the top of the mountain, Abraham placed Isaac on top of the altar! He then took the knife to kill his son. But suddenly he heard God's voice.

Voice of God: Do not harm him. I know that you fear God because you did not hold anything back, not even the son you love.

Narrator: Abraham found a ram caught in a bush by its horns. He knew that this was the animal to be sacrificed. Abraham called the place "The-Lord-Will-Provide."

Isaac

The Promise Explained
♫ Genesis 18:1-15 ♫

Memory Verse

Is anything too hard for the Lord?

~Genesis 18:14

What You Need

• page 17
• pencils

What to Do

Duplicate page 17 and give one to each child. Show the students how to use the code to complete the story. Once the children complete the story, let them take turns reading the paragraphs aloud.

What to Say

Explain to the children that before Isaac was born, his parents, Abraham and Sarah, did not believe that they would ever have children even though God said they would. Sarah had been unable to have children. When God first came to Abraham with His plan, Abraham was 75 years old and Sarah was 65 — too old to have a baby. Abraham and Sarah thought that having a baby at their age was too difficult. Is there something you have to do that you think is too difficult? Let's ask God for help. (Pray.)

Code Story

Use the Morse code below to complete the story.

A	B	C	D	E	F	G	H	I
•-	-•••	•••	-••	•	••-•	--•	••••	••

J	K	L	M	N	O	P	Q	R
-•-•	-•-	—	--	-•	⋮	••••	••-•	•-•

S	T	U	V	W	X	Y	Z
•••	-	••-	•••-	•--	-••-	-•--	--••

Abraham was `-•` `••` `-•` `•` `-` `•• ••` - `-•` `••` `-•` `•`

_____ _____ _____ _____ _____ _____ - _____ _____ _____ _____ years old.

His wife Sarah was `•` `••` `--•` `••••` `-` `•• ••` - `-•` `••` `-•` `•`

_____ _____ _____ _____ _____ _____ - _____ _____ _____ _____

years old.

For a long time, they could not have `•• •` `••••` `••` `——` `-••` `• ••` `•` `-•`

_____ _____ _____ _____ _____ _____ _____ _____ .

Years ago, God had promised Abraham they would have a child. But the child had not come.

One day, some men came to visit Abraham. Abraham rushed to get them something to eat. He did not

know that the men were `•-` `-•` `--•` `•` `——` `•••`

_____ _____ _____ _____ _____ _____ .

"Where is Sarah, your wife?" they asked Abraham. "In the tent," he replied.
The Lord had a message for Abraham. "I will return to you this time next year. Your wife Sarah will have a

`•••` `⋮` `-•`

_____ _____ _____ .

When Sarah heard what was said, she could not help but `——` `•-` `••-` `--•` `••••`

_____ _____ _____ _____ _____ .

Me? Have a child at my age? she wondered.
The Lord knew what she had been thinking. "Why did Sarah laugh? Is anything too hard for God? I will return next year. Sarah will have a son."
Sarah did not want to admit that she had laughed. But she had. Still God planned to keep His promise. He always keeps His promises.

17

Isaac

The Promise Is Given
✎ Genesis 12:2-3; 15:1-5; 17:1-8, 15-19 ✎

Memory Verse

Sons are a heritage from the Lord, children a reward from him.
~Psalm 127:3

What You Need

• duplicated page
• crayons or markers

What to Do

Photocopy this page and give one to each child. Explain that they should color only the spaces with vowels.

What to Say

Children are always important to their families, but Bible-time children were especially valued by Bible-time parents. People who could not have children felt embarrassed. Imagine how Abraham and Sarah, two people who followed God, felt to be childless for so long! But one day, Abraham received an important message from God that he and Sarah would have a baby even though they were old. The baby's name was Isaac. What is the most important promise you've ever been given? Did that promise come true? How did you feel?

Ishmael

God Hears Ishmael
🔊 Genesis 21:8-21 🔊

Memory Verse

For the Lord comforts his people and will have compassion on his afflicted ones.

~Isaiah 49:13

What You Need

• pages 19-21
• felt
• scissors
• fabric glue
• markers
• Bible map

What to Do

Copy the story below and pages 20-21 for each child. The children can work together to make two puppets to show the action of the story as they take turns reading it. Show how to use the patterns to cut out two pieces of felt with each pattern. Then they should glue the pieces together, leaving an opening at the bottom of each for their hand like a glove. The students can use extra felt and markers to make the puppets look like Hagar and Ishmael. Before the children act out the story, help them locate Beersheba on a map. Explain that a desert surrounded this city.

What to Say

Having waited and waited for God to give them a child, Abraham and Sarah were frustrated and disappointed. So Abraham had a baby with another woman. His name was Ishmael. But that was also when the trouble started. Soon Sarah became pregnant as God promised. When her baby Isaac was born, she did not want Ishmael and his mother Hagar around anymore. They were sent to wander the desert near Beersheba. Hagar felt forgotten. Like Hagar, we can sometimes feel forgotten. But God never forgets anyone.

Hagar's and Ishmael's Story

Ishmael and Isaac were Abraham's sons. They had different mothers. Ishmael's mother was Hagar, Sarah's maid. Sarah was Isaac's mother. Sarah and Hagar did not get along. One day Sarah heard Ishmael making fun of Isaac. Sarah told Abraham, "Send Hagar and Ishmael away. I don't want them to share in Isaac's inheritance."

Abraham did not want to send Ishmael away. But God told Abraham, "Do what Sarah says. Through Isaac you will have many descendants. But I will also make a great nation of Ishmael, since he is your son too."

Abraham prepared food and water for Hagar and Ishmael. Hagar took her son to the desert. They wandered around, not knowing where to go.

Soon the water ran out. Hagar left her son by a bush and walked some distance away. She was afraid that both she and Ishmael would die.

Ishmael cried too. God heard Ishmael's cries. An angel spoke to Hagar. "Hagar, what's the matter? Do not be afraid! God heard your son crying. Go and comfort Ishmael. One day he will be a great nation."

God allowed Hagar to see what she hadn't seen before: a well! She filled her water container and gave some to Ishmael to drink. They lived in the desert of Paran, where Ishmael grew up.

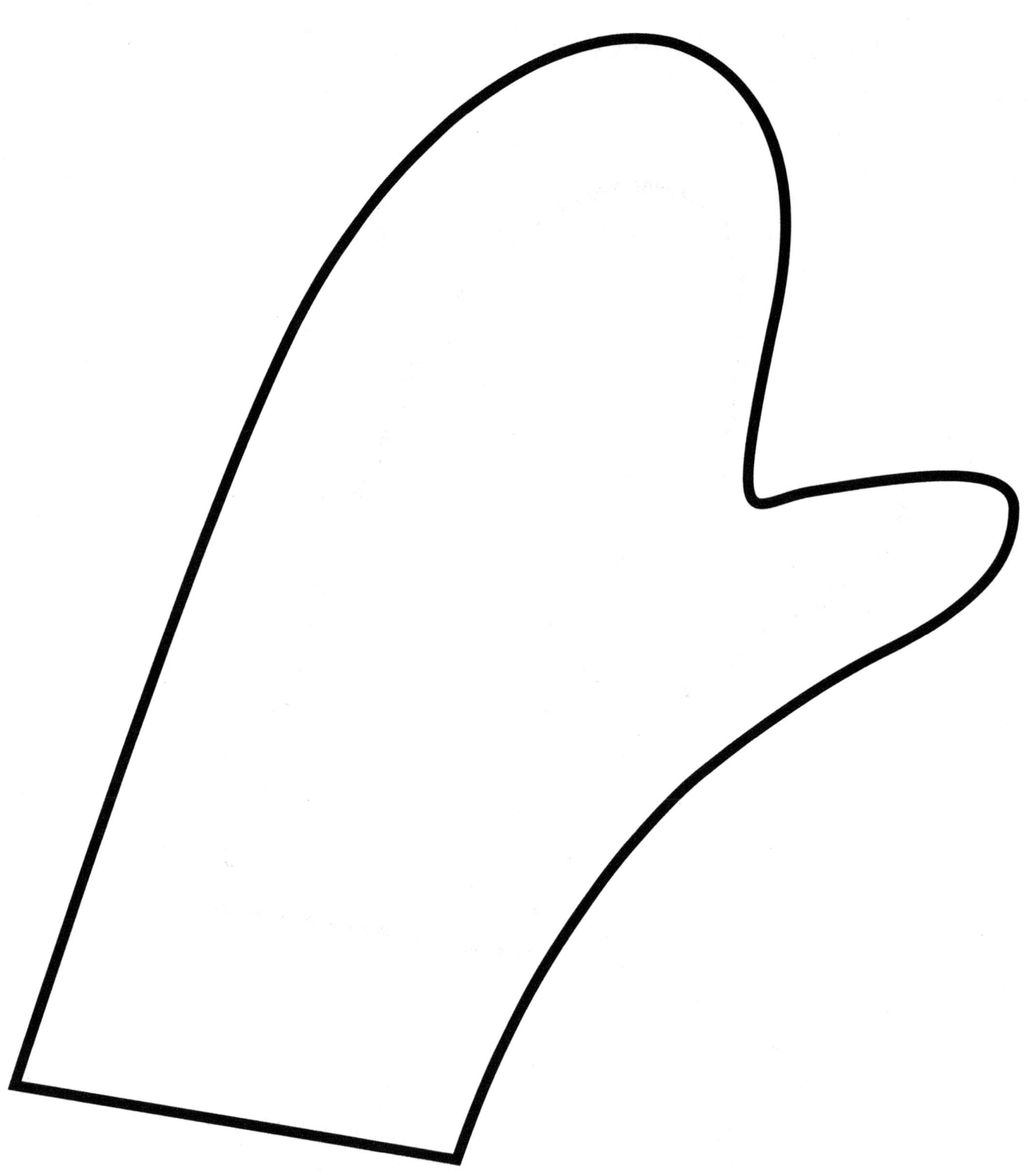

Jacob and Esau

Keep the Peace!
∽ Genesis 25:19-34 ∽

Memory Verse

If it is possible, as far as it depends on you, live at peace with everyone.

~Romans 12:18

What You Need

• pages 22 and 23
• scissors
• tape
• crayons
• pencils

What to Do

Duplicate this page and page 23. Let the children take turns reading from Genesis 25:19-34 in their Bibles. Write the memory verse on the chalkboard for the children to copy. Give each child a copy of the folder and the four "promissory" notes. Explain that a promissory note is what people sign when they promise to pay something. Have the students cut out the pieces. They should fold the paper along the dashed lines to assemble the folder with pockets. They should tape the ends of the squares in the middle to secure the pockets. They can use the folder to store the notes. On the figures, they can write a note to someone they care about, telling the person what they will do to "live at peace" with him or her. They can draw themselves on the other side of the figures. After a few weeks have the students bring back their folders to class and tell what they did to keep their promises.

What to Say

When Isaac grew up, he married Rebekah. For a while, they couldn't have children, just like his parents Abraham and Isaac. But Isaac prayed and God gave them twins — Jacob and Esau. God declared that they represented two future nations. But the two "nations" were at war, even while being born! And they were certainly different. They fought a lot and terrible things happened because of their fighting. Fighting never solves anything.

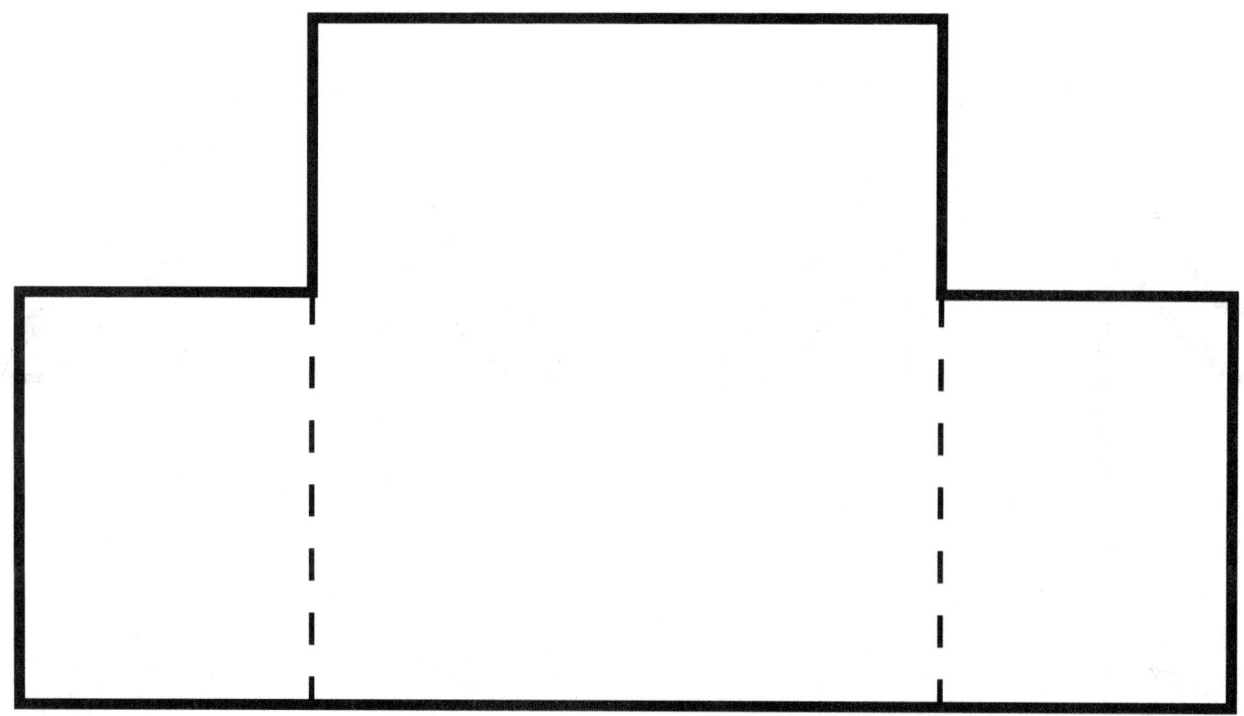

Joseph

A Colorful Coat
ꙮ Genesis 37 ꙮ

Memory Verse

God does not show favoritism but accepts men from every nation who fear him and do what is right.
~Acts 10:34-35

What You Need

- page 25
- heavy paper
- fabric and felt scraps
- scissors
- glue

What to Do

Photocopy page 25 on heavy paper for each child. Have the children design a multicolored coat using the pattern and fabric scraps.

What to Say

Jacob gave Joseph a colorful coat to show Joseph how much he was loved. This coat was a tunic with long sleeves. Joseph was the only one in his family to have a coat like this. The coat showed that Joseph was Jacob's favorite son. How do your parents show their love for you? How does God show His love for you?

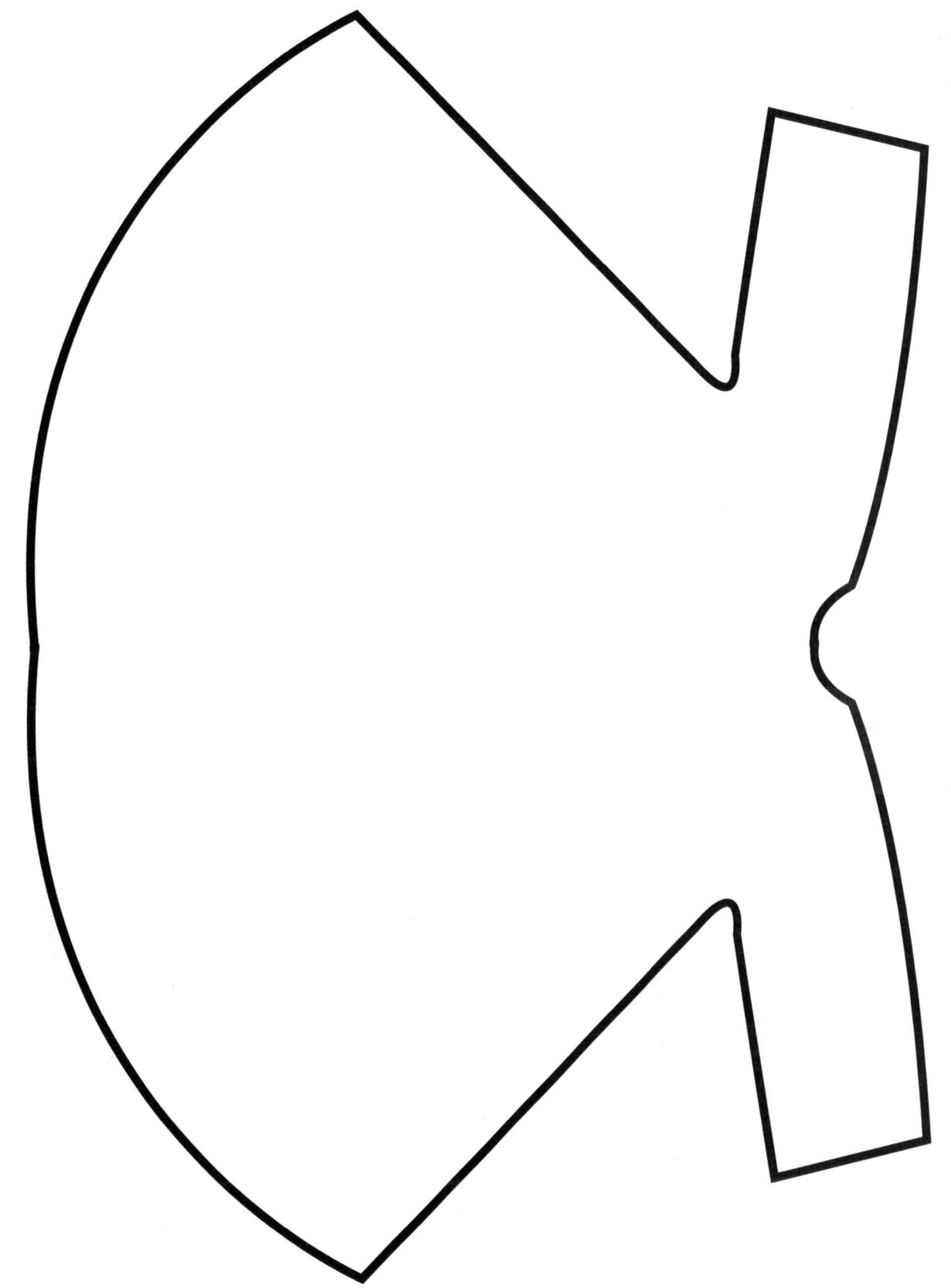

Joseph

The Favorite Son
ᔆᵒ Genesis 37 ᵒᔆ

Memory Verse

God does not show favoritism but accepts men from every nation who fear him and do what is right.
~Acts 10:34-35

What You Need

• page 27
• pencils
• Bibles

What to Do

Give each child a copy of the puzzle. Help the children fill in the crossword using an NIV Bible. The answers are on page 95.

Introduction

Jacob, Isaac's son, had 12 sons. Joseph was Isaac's favorite son because Joseph was also the son of Rachel, the wife Jacob loved most. This did not make for a happy home! Joseph's brothers disliked Joseph. Knowing that Joseph was the favorite made the other brothers feel bad. Have you ever been in a situation where someone else was the favorite? How did you feel? As our memory verse tells us, God does not play favorites. He loves everyone.

Joseph Crossword

Across

1. Joseph was _____'s favorite son (37:3).
3. Joseph was about _____ years old (37:2).
6. Joseph's brothers wanted to sell Joseph as a _____ (37:25-27).

Down

1. Joseph's brothers were _____ of all the attention Joseph received (37:4).
2. Joseph was given a special _____ with many colors (37:2).
4. Joseph's brothers called Joseph "the _____" (37:19).
5. _____ tried to stop his brothers from hurting Joseph (37:21).

Miriam

Baby in the Water
∽ Exodus 2:1-10 ∾

Memory Verse

Be still and know that I am God.

~Psalm 46:10

What You Need

- page 29
- blue paper
- tape
- doll
- basket

What to Do

Photocopy page 29. Designate an area of your classroom where the children can act out the play. Divide this area in two sections: a "home" and the Nile River. Tape several strips of blue paper on the floor to represent the Nile River. Have a doll and a basket large enough to hold the doll.

What to Say

The Hebrew people had lived in Egypt for hundreds of years. They had multiplied, to the disgust of Pharaoh. Pharaoh's decree to kill all the Hebrew baby boys could not stop God. God's plans to rescue His future deliverer were in the hands of a small girl and her mother. Jochebed, Moses' mother, hid her precious young son, Moses. When she could hide him no longer, she made a basket and placed him inside. She sent her daughter Miriam to watch over the basket as it floated down the Nile River.

Miriam and Moses

Characters
- narrator
- Amram
- Jochebed
- Miriam
- Pharaoh's daughter
- a servant

Narrator: The pharaoh of Egypt was worried. The Hebrew people in the land of Egypt had become a large nation of people. So Pharaoh made the people slaves. But that didn't stop their nation from growing. Pharaoh decided to kill all of the Hebrew baby boys. One day, a man from the house of Levi and his wife discovered that God had given them a son. The man's name was Amram. His wife's name was Jochebed.

Amram and Jochebed enter the home section. Jochebed carries the doll.

Amram: Who would have thought that the birth of such a fine son could bring me such sorrow? *Jochebed holding doll:* He is beautiful, isn't he? We must hide him from Pharaoh's soldiers. We can't let them hurt our son.

Amram and Jochebed exit.

Narrator: The family kept the baby hidden for three months. Finally, they could hide him no longer.

Jochebed and Miriam enter. Miriam carries the doll.

Miriam: What shall we do, Mother?

Jochebed: We must send the baby away. Perhaps God will see that he gets safely away. Get a basket for me.

Miriam hands Jochebed a basket.

Jochebed: Help me make it waterproof.

Miriam: What will you do with the basket?

Jochebed: We'll put the baby inside. Then, I want you to set the basket in the Nile River. Watch over it while it floats. Let me know what happens to it. *Clutches Miriam's hand.* Don't let anything bad happen to your brother, Miriam. I'm counting on you.

Miriam takes the basket and sets it in the Nile. Soon, Pharaoh's daughter enters along with her servant.

Pharaoh's daughter: That's strange. There's a basket over there in the river. Get it for me.
The servant girl picks up the basket and brings it to Pharaoh's daughter.
Pharaoh's daughter takes doll out: This is one of the Hebrew babies!

Miriam: Shall I find a Hebrew woman to act as a nurse for the baby?

Pharaoh's daughter: That is a good idea. Go. Take the child with you. *Hands Miriam the basket and doll.* Tell the woman you find that I will pay her to care for this baby.

Miriam runs to the "Home" section where Jochebed waits.

Miriam: Mother! Mother!

Jochebed: Why have you brought the basket back?

Miriam: The daughter of Pharaoh found it. She wants you to take care of the baby until he's old enough to go and live with her.

Jochebed: Praise the God of Abraham, Isaac and Jacob!

Narrator: So Jochebed was able to take care of her own son. When he was older, she took the child to Pharaoh's daughter. Pharaoh's daughter named the child Moses, which means "to draw out." She named him this because she had drawn him out of the Nile.

Miriam

Our Helper
℘ Exodus 2:1-10 ℘

Memory Verse

Be still, and know that I am God.

~Psalm 46:10

What You Need

• duplicated page
• crayons

What to Do

Give each student a copy of this page. They should look for and color the letter shapes. When they have finished shading the shapes, remind them of the memory verse on page 19 (Isaiah 49:13) in the lesson about Ishmael.

What to Say

Miriam was a Hebrew girl living in Egypt. At that time, the Hebrew people were slaves. The king of the land — Pharaoh — did not want the Hebrew population to grow. So he ordered that all of the Hebrew baby boys should be killed. Miriam had a baby brother named Moses. Moses' mother wanted Moses to be safe. So she put him in a basket on the Nile. Miriam stood by the river to make sure that Moses was safe. That's how God is. He stands by you to make sure you're safe, too.

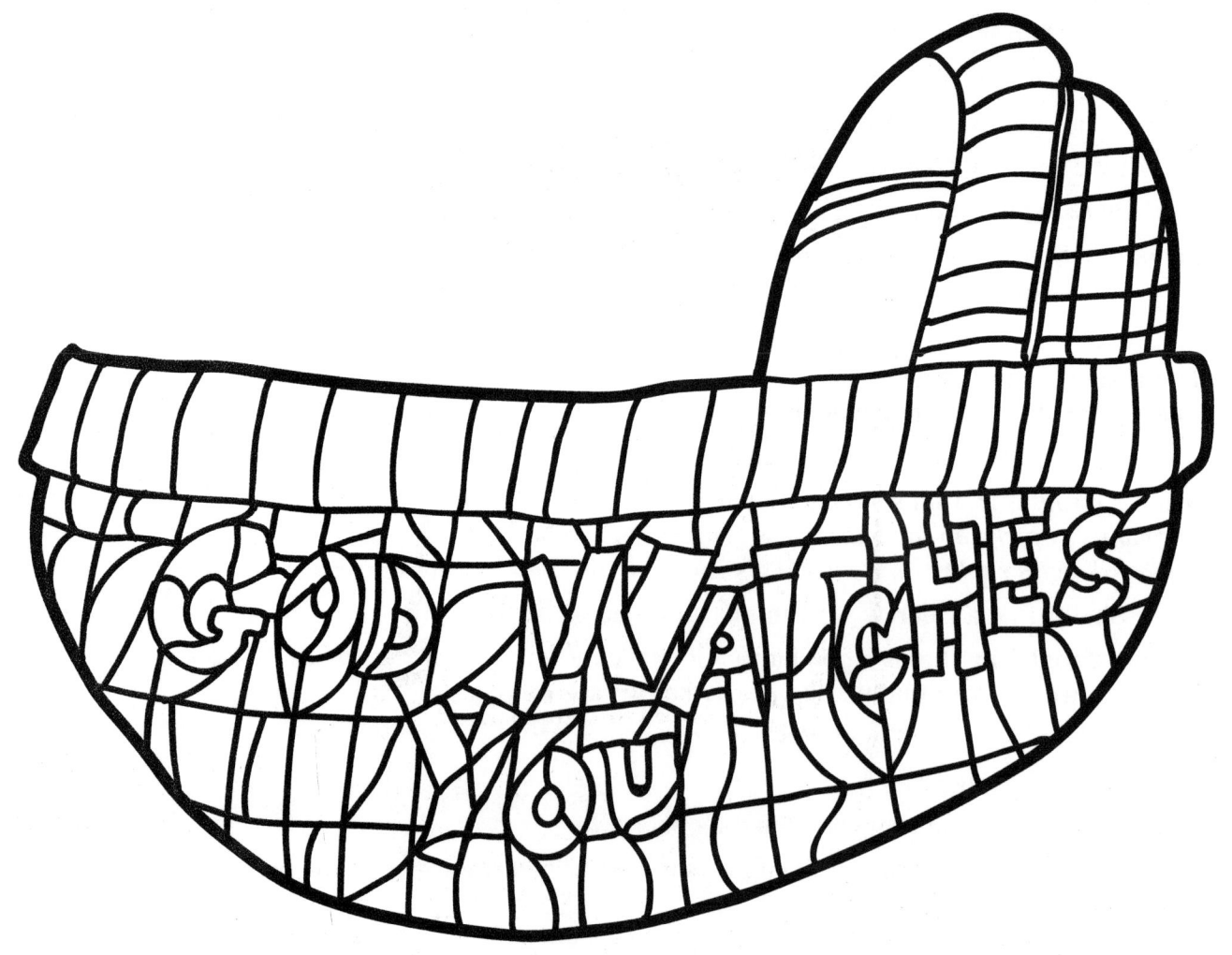

Samuel

God Calls Samuel
1 Samuel 3:1-21

Memory Verse

I praise you, Father, Lord of heaven and earth, because you have hidden these things from the wise and learned, and revealed them to little children.
~Luke 10:21

What You Need

- page 32
- tape player
- cassette tape

What to Do

Have the students perform the script on page 32 as a pretend radio drama. The drama can be performed sitting down, but encourage your readers to be dramatic. Use sound effects. For example, rap a wooden block against a piece of tile or against another block to make the sound of footsteps. (The sound does not have to be exactly like real footsteps.) Tape the performance and play it back for the class.

What to Say

Samuel was Hannah's son. Hannah had given her son to the Lord to serve Him in the temple. Eli the priest watched over the boy. One night, Samuel thought he heard someone call him. Was it Eli? Or was it someone else?

A Voice in the Night

Characters
- Narrator
- God
- Samuel
- Eli

Narrator: WKLZ presents "A Voice in the Night," a radio drama. As our story opens, Samuel is asleep in the temple. Suddenly he hears a mysterious voice.

God: Samuel! Samuel!

Samuel sleepily: That must be Eli.

Make the sound of footsteps.

Samuel: Here I am, Eli. Here I am. You called me.

Eli sleepily: I didn't call you. Go back to bed.

Make the sound of footsteps.

God: Samuel! Samuel!

Make the sound of footsteps.

Samuel: Here I am. You called me.

Eli: My son, I did not call. Go back and lie down.

Make the sound of footsteps.

God: Samuel! Samuel!

Samuel: Here I am. You called me.

Eli: It is the Lord. Go and lie down. If He calls you again, say, "Speak, Lord, for your servant is listening."

Make the sound of footsteps.

God: Samuel! Samuel!

Samuel: Speak, Lord, for your servant is listening.

God: I am about to do something to surprise everyone in Israel. Eli's sons have sinned. I told him I would judge his family. That is what will happen.

Narrator: Samuel finally went to sleep. He did not want to tell Eli what he had heard. But Eli knew God had spoken to Samuel.

Eli: Don't keep back anything that God has told you.

Narrator: So, Samuel told Eli everything. And God did exactly what He said He would do. Eli's sons were put to death. Samuel learned to respect God's Word. God was with Samuel as he grew up.

32

Samuel

Hannah Asks for a Son
♪ 1 Samuel 1 ♪

Memory Verse

Ask and it will be given to you; seek and you will find; knock and the door will be opened to you.
~Luke 11:9

What You Need

• duplicated page

What to Do

Teach the children to sign the words shown below. Read through the poem once, to know where the signs should be used. Then practice using the signs.

What to Say

Hannah was very sad. Hannah and her husband Elkanah wanted to have a son. But Hannah couldn't have any children. What was Hannah to do? She did the only thing she knew how to do: she went to God. And that was the best thing she could have done! Even though God encourages us to pray, we don't necessarily get everything we ask for. He knows what is best for us.

Signs and Rhymes

Use the hand motions below as your take turns reading the poem.

Son

God   **Sad**

Hannah wanted to have a son. (*use the sign for son*)

She prayed to God (*use the sign for God*) to give her one.

She went to the tabernacle one day.

It was there that she wanted to pray. (*fold hands*)

"If you give me a son (*use the sign for son*), as I'm asking You to.

I promise he will be a worker for You.

"His hair won't be cut. This I vow.

Please hear me, Lord, (*use the sign for God*) as I pray now."

Eli the priest had been around.

He saw her lips move without any sound.

He thought she was drunk instead of in prayer. (*fold hands*)

He told her off then and there.

"I'm sad, not drunk," Hannah replied.

"I can't have a child (*use the sign for son*), although I've tried."

"I've told the Lord (*use the sign for God*) how I feel.

I've poured out my heart, because my sorrow is real."

"Go in peace," Eli said. "May God (*use the sign for God*) do as you ask.

You can always trust Him with any task."

When God (*use the sign for God*) gave her a son (*use the sign for son*), Hannah was glad.

It was hard to believe she had ever been sad (*use the sign for sad*).

David

David Fights Goliath
✄ 1 Samuel 17 ✄

Memory Verse

"Not by might nor by power, but by my Spirit," *says the Lord.*
~Zechariah 4:6

What You Need

- page 35
- pencils

What to Do

Duplicate page 35 for each student. Explain that in Bible times armies would each send a champion. The champions would fight each other, rather than the armies having to clash. Give each student a copy of the code puzzle. Explain that semaphore is a code used by railroad workers to pass information. After students complete the code, let them take turns reading the story aloud.

What to Say

What do you do when you're facing a giant problem? The Israelites' "giant" problem was a giant named Goliath! But God had a champion ready to face this giant. The champion was not a mighty warrior with lots of combat training. No, the champion was a shepherd who believed the real champion was God Himself.

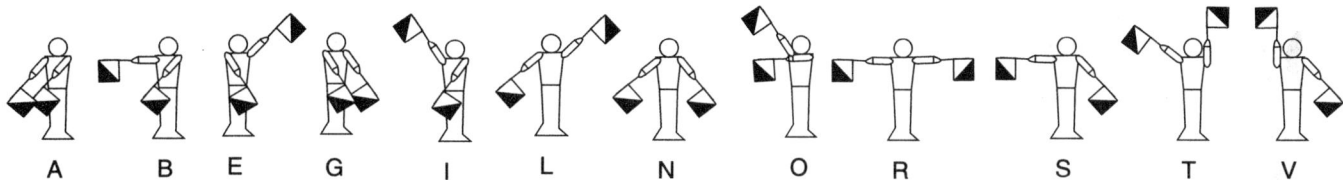

The Philistines were enemies of the people of Israel. The armies of both nations went to war and camped near each other. One of the Philistines' soldiers was named Goliath. Goliath was over

NINE

_____ _____ _____ _____

feet tall. His armor alone weighed over one hundred pounds!

Every day for forty days, Goliath went to the Israelites' camp. "Choose a man to fight me," he said with a sneer. "If I win, my people will be your

SERVANTS

_____ _____ _____ _____ _____ _____ _____ _____.

If you win, your people will be our

SERVANTS

_____ _____ _____ _____ _____ _____ _____ ____.

He then made fun of Israel. King Saul and the Israelites were afraid of Goliath. They didn't believe anyone could beat him. One day, David went to visit three of his brothers in the Israelites' camp. He heard what Goliath had to say.

"See how he comes out to insult Israel?" one of the soldiers told David. "The king promises to reward the man who kills him."

"Who is this man that he would dare insult the army of God?" David said.

David's brother

ELIAB

_____ _____ _____ _____

heard what David said. "Why are

you here?" he asked. "Who's taking care of that little flock of yours while you're here? You're just

ARROGANT

_____ _____ _____ _____ _____ _____ _____ _____

"

"Why are you mad at me?" David asked. "Why can't I talk?"

Saul soon sent for David. He wanted to know if David really wanted to fight Goliath.

"Yes, I will fight Goliath for you," David said.

"Then may the Lord go with you," Saul said. He gave David his own armor to take into battle.

"I can't wear this," David said. "I've never used it before."

Instead he picked up five

STONES

_____ _____ _____ _____ _____ _____

from a stream and put them in his

shepherd's bag. With his slingshot in hand, he went to face Goliath. Goliath soon appeared with his shield bearer in front. He looked at David. David was only a youth. "Do you think I'm a dog that you come to me with sticks?" Goliath asked, mockingly.

David wasn't afraid. "I come to you in the name of the Lord."

David ran to met Goliath. He stuck a stone in his sling and whirled it around his head. The stone flew through the air and struck Goliath. Goliath fell over dead. God had won the battle!

David

David Is Anointed King
🎝 1 Samuel 16:7 🎝

Memory Verse

The Lord does not look at the things man looks at. Man looks at the outward appearance, but the Lord looks at the heart.

~1 Samuel 16:7

What You Need

- page 37
- felt
- pens
- fabric glue
- hole punch

What to Do

Give each student a copy of the finger puppet pattern. Show how to trace the pattern twice on felt and cut out the patterns. Go around and punch eye holes on one pattern for each child. Have the students glue the puppet together along the edges, being careful to leave the bottom open. Allow to dry. Have the students use the finger puppets to tell the story of David's anointing below (some can be Samuel and some David). Encourage your students to perform the puppet show for a group of younger children! (After David is revealed as the new king-to-be, explain to the children that David was probably just a teenager.)

What to Say

God sometimes uses small people to carry out His great plans. Those great plans included anointing someone to take Saul's place as king of Israel. But who? The prophet Samuel was sent to Bethlehem to the family of a man named Jesse. Jesse had eight sons. One of them would be the new king. Would it be tall, handsome Eliab, Jesse's oldest son? Or would it be someone else?

David Is Anointed

Saul had sinned. So God told Samuel that Saul would no longer be king of Israel.

"Go to Jesse in Bethlehem," God said. "Anoint the one I point out."

So Samuel did as God told him. As soon as Samuel saw Jesse's son Eliab, he thought he had found the one to anoint. Eliab was tall and good looking.

But the Lord said, "Don't consider him because of his looks or how tall he is. He is not the one I want. The Lord does not look at the way a man looks on the outside. The Lord looks at the heart."

Jesse called seven of his sons. Samuel looked at all of them, but the Lord chose none of them.

Samuel asked Jesse, "Have you any more sons?"

"Just the youngest," said Jesse. "He's out with the sheep."

Samuel said, "Send for him."

So Jesse sent for his youngest son David. David was good looking too. But he was just a youth.

The Lord said, "Rise and anoint him. He is the one."

Samuel poured oil on David's head. One day David would be the new king.

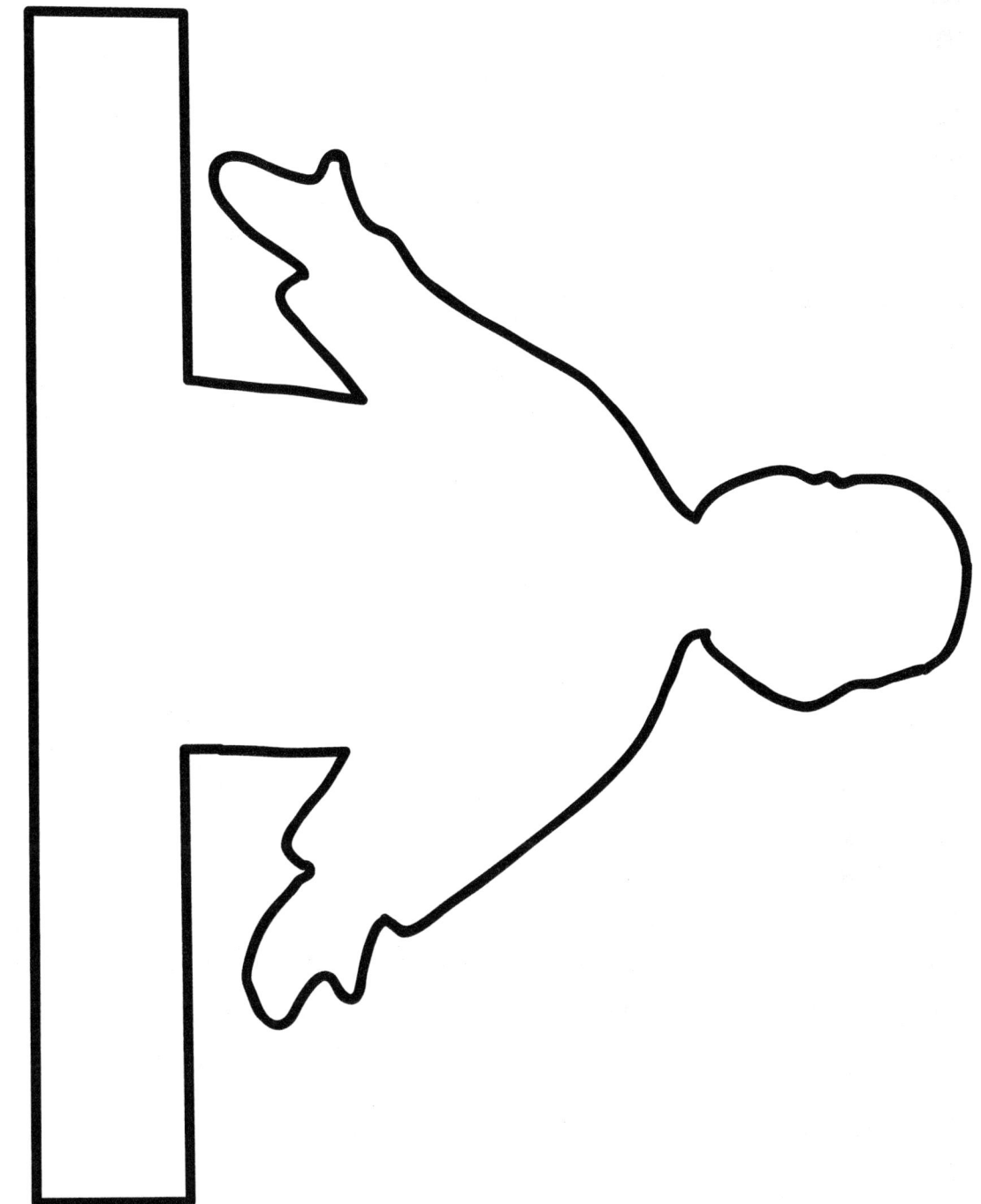

David

Pals for Life
♪ 1 Samuel 18:1-4 ♫

Memory Verse

A friend loves at all times.

~Proverbs 17:17

What You Need

• duplicated page
• pencils

What to Do

Give each student a copy of this page. Select two to read 1 Samuel 18:1-4 aloud. Ask the students to describe the kind of friend they think Jonathan was. Then discuss the slogan "What would Jesus do?" (WWJD), which reminds us to act like Jesus (they've probably seen it on bracelets). Have the students create and write a slogan in the box below that would show how to be a friend who loves at all times. Then they can use the slogan's initials to make a WWJD bracelet on the blank one. For example: AWLF (Always Willing to Love a Friend).

What to Say

Do you have a best friend? David had one. His name was Jonathan. Jonathan was King Saul's son. David was just a shepherd. But Jonathan didn't care. David was his friend. Are you that kind of friend? How would your friends describe you?

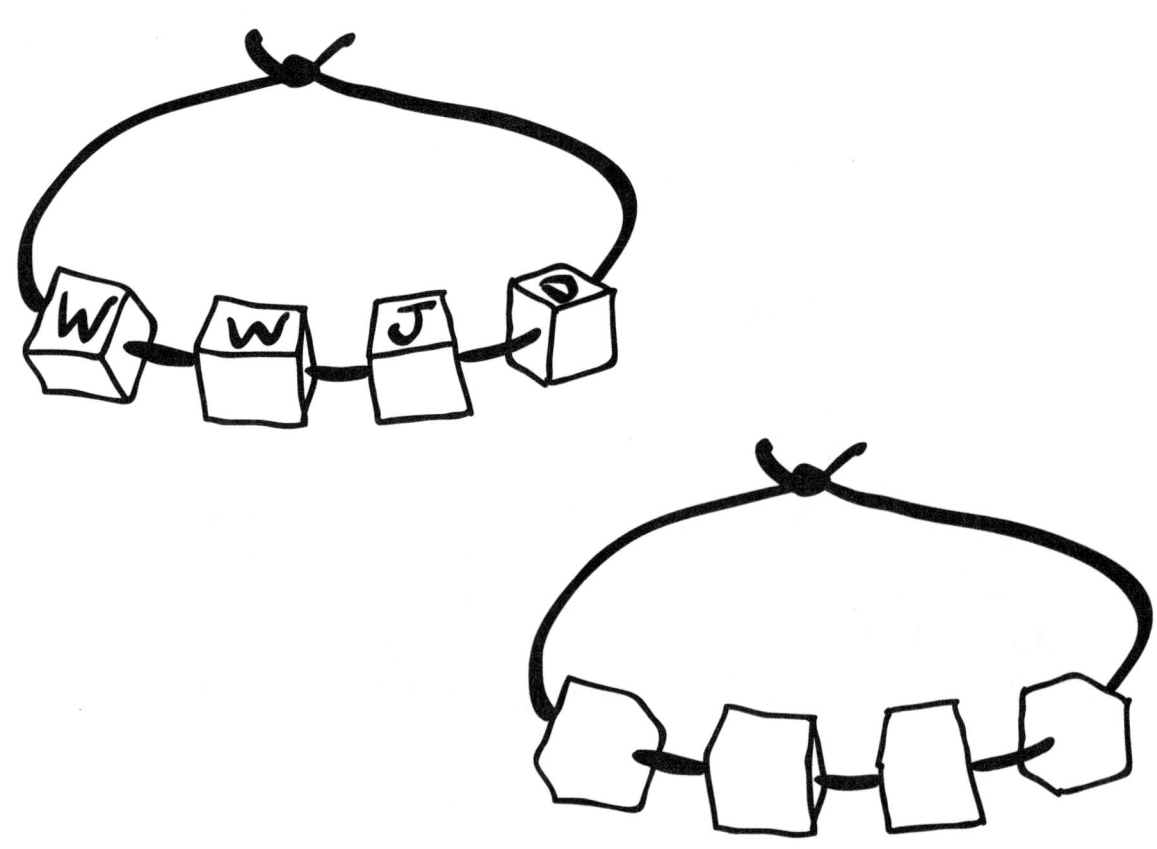

The Widow of Zarephath's Son

Back from the Dead
♪ 1 Kings 17:14-24 ♫

Memory Verse

Without faith it is impossible to please God.
~Hebrews 11:6

What You Need

• blanket

What to Do

Let the students take turns reading 1 Kings 17:14-24 aloud from their Bibles. Afterward, to test their comprehension of the action of the story, let them pantomime the story without using words. Select volunteers to be the widow, her son and Elijah. Lay a blanket on the floor. The student playing the son should pantomime a sudden illness, then lie on the blanket. The "widow" should run to get "Elijah." Instead of having Elijah stretch across the child playing the son, have your Elijah kneel by him as if praying to the Lord to heal him. When Elijah grabs the son's hand, that is your actor's signal to come back to life. You can have more than one group of students act out the story.

What to Say

Elijah helped a widow and her son in the town of Zarephath. Trouble had once more come to that family. The widow's only son suddenly died. What was she to do? Accordingly to Elijah, there was only one thing to do: trust God. Do you think the widow had faith in God when she went to Elijah? Why or why not? How did Elijah show that he had faith in God? Why do you think faith pleases God?

The Widow of Zarephath's Son

Saving a Widow's Son
✧1 Kings 17:7-14✧

Memory Verse

Do not worry about your life…. Look at the birds of the air; they do not sow or reap or store away in barns, and yet your heavenly Father feeds them.

~Matthew 6:25-26

What You Need

• duplicated page
• pencils

What to Do

Photocopy this page for each student. Have the students take turns reading aloud sections of the story of the widow of Zarephath in 1 Kings 17:7-24. Then have the students work through the maze. Explain that in Bible times, widows were among the poorest people. Many widows depended on their children to support them in their older years.

What to Say

When Ahab was king of Israel, he led the people to worship idols. God was angry at the bad things that Ahab had done. So there was no rain on earth for a few years. There was little food. After using ravens to feed the prophet Elijah, God sent him to help a widow and her son in Zarephath. This widow feared for her life and for that of her son. They had nearly run out of food. But God had not forgotten them.

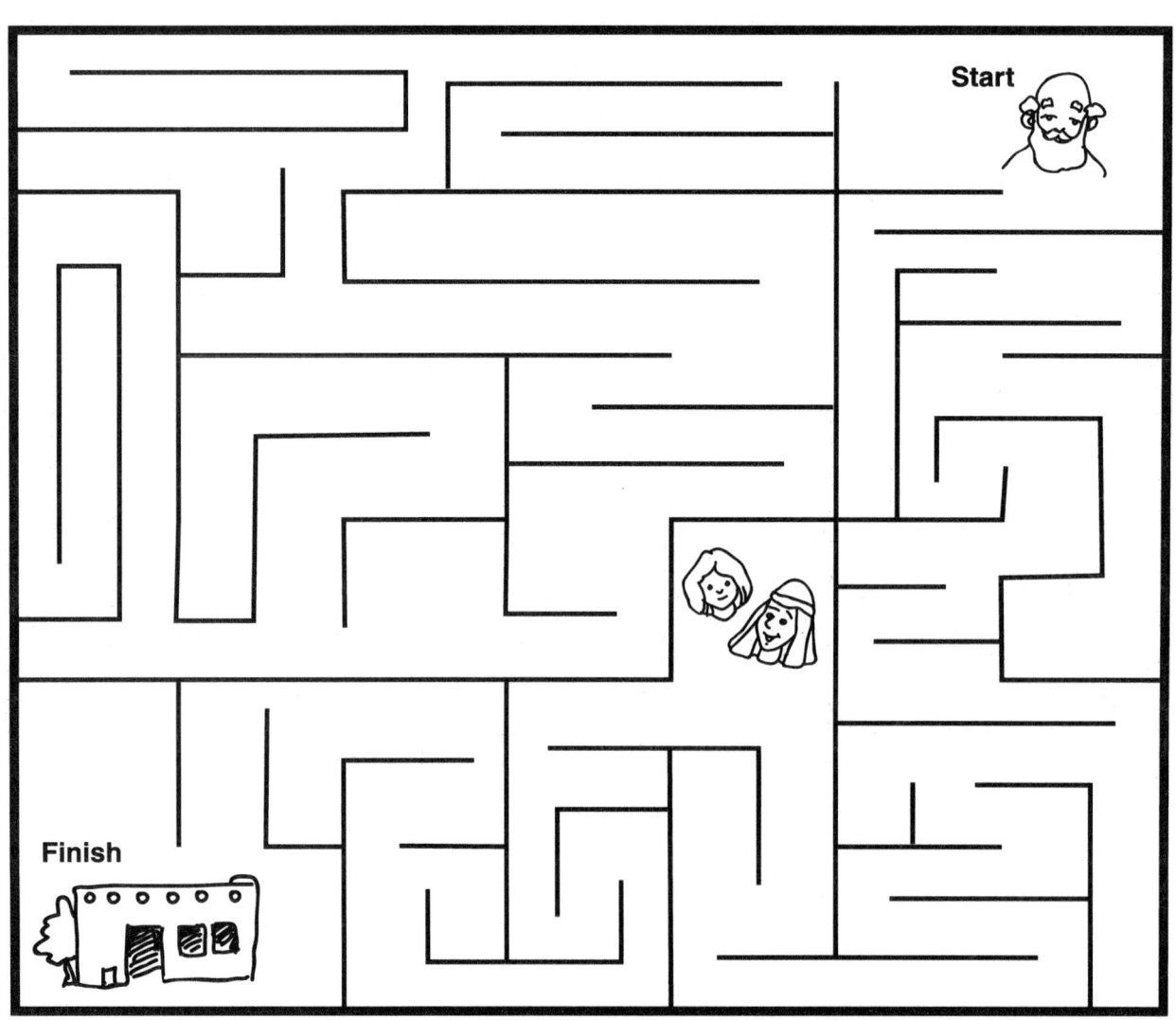

Start

Finish

The Widow's Sons

Elisha Helps the Widow
♪ 2 Kings 4:1-7 ♫

Memory Verse

The Lord watches over the alien and sustains the fatherless and the widow, but he frustrates the ways of the wicked.

~Psalm 146:9

What You Need

• no materials needed

What to Do

Have the students take turns reading the story (2 Kings 4:1-7) aloud from their Bibles. To test their comprehension, play the Bible review game below. All students can be contestants and they may choose from either category. Read the clue from the answer column, then instruct the students that they must respond in the form of a question. They must raise their hands to guess. Whoever raises his or her hand first gets to answer.

What to Say

Elisha was the prophet who took over when Elijah was taken to heaven. Elisha was sent to help a widow. This widow had been married to a prophet. Like the widow of Zarephath, this widow was poor and had little food. All she had were her two sons and a little oil. The husband of the widow of this story owed money before he died. The person he owed money to threatened to take her sons away as slaves. Poor people in Israel sometimes sold themselves in slavery to pay their debts. But without her sons to support her later in life, the widow would probably starve to death.

People

Answer	Question
This prophet was sent to help a woman in need.	Who is Elisha?
This person needed help from God's prophet.	Who is the widow?
Two was all the widow had.	What are sons?
The widow owed money, so the person she owed threatened to take this from her.	What are her sons?

Things

Answer	Question
The widow had only a little of this liquid.	What is oil?
Elisha told the widow to borrow a lot of these.	What are jars?
Elisha told the widow to borrow from these people.	Who are neighbors?
Elisha told the widow to go inside and shut this.	What is the door?
Elisha told the widow this could be used to pay her debts.	What is the oil?

The Widow's Sons

Memory Verse

The Lord watches over the alien and sustains the fatherless and the widow, but he frustrates the ways of the wicked.
~Psalm 146:9

What You Need

• duplicated page
• pens

What to Do

Explain to the students that the Israelites had many laws about helping widows, orphans and aliens (strangers). Students can do a service project to help those in need. You can structure this in one of two ways: 1. Look for ways kids can serve in your church. Provide your church's bulletins or ministry lists. Help the students choose an area in which they can serve. Students can serve together as a class or in pairs. Suggest a minimum and a maximum amount of time to devote to the project, depending on your students' interests. (Examples: nursery, food pantry, usher, church office.) 2. Look for ways students can serve at home, in their neighborhoods or at school. (Examples: a clean-up project, adopt an elderly person, tutor.) Copy the pledge card below, one per student. This pledge card is like a promissory note. By filling it out and signing it, the student is promising to serve.

What to Say

The prophet Elisha was willing to help a widow and her two sons. God gives us the ability to help others too. Use this pledge as your promise to help someone.

PLEDGE OF SERVICE

NAME _____

I PROMISE TO: _____

_____

FOR _____ WEEKS

The Shunammite's Son

Kindness from Strangers
♫ 2 Kings 4:8-37 ♫

Memory Verse

Those who know your name will trust in you, for you, Lord, have never forsaken those who seek you.

~Psalm 9:10

What You Need

• page 44
• pens

What to Do

Copy the puzzle on page 44 for each child. Assist them in filling in the answers. The answers are on page 95.

What to Say

Elisha had received food and a room from a woman in Shunem. Now he wanted to do something for her in return. He knew what the best gift would be: a son. Imagine being given such a wonderful gift! Now imagine having that gift suddenly taken away. Remember how especially important children were in Bible times and how Abraham and Sarah and Hannah felt? How would you feel? The women from Shunem felt terrible! But God had a surprise for her.

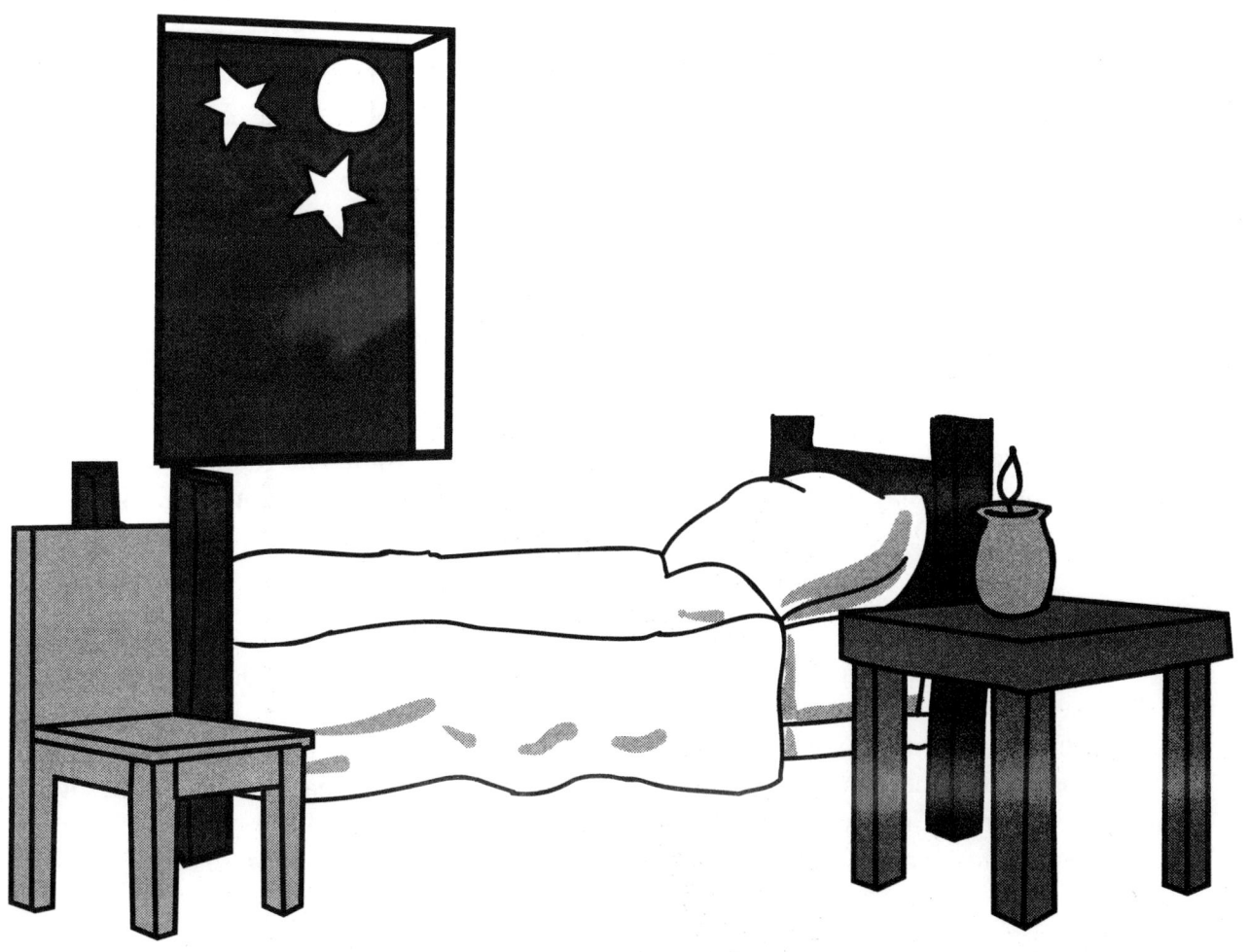

The Shunammite's Son

Across

1. The Shunammite woman provided this man of God with a room and food. (2 Kings 4:8)
2. This servant of 1 Across told the man of God that the woman had no son. (2 Kings 4:14)
3. The woman was _____ to believe that Elisha was telling the truth. (2 Kings 4:16)

Down

4. The son of the Shunammite complained of pain in his _____ one day. (2 Kings 4:19)
5. Before anyone knew it, the boy had _____. (2 Kings 4:20)
6. The Shunammite went to 1 Across's home on Mount _____. (2 Kings 4:25)
7. 1 Across told 2 Across to lay this on the boy's face. But nothing happened. (2 Kings 4:29)
8. 1 Across went to the house and _____ to the Lord. (2 Kings 4:33)
9. After stretching across the boy, he came back to _____. (2 Kings 4:35)

The Shunammite's Son

Trusted to Help
2 Kings 4:8-37

Memory Verse

Those who know your name will trust in you, for you, Lord, have never forsaken those who seek you.

~Psalm 9:10

What You Need

• duplicated page
• pencils

What to Do

Give each student a copy of this page. Use it to help your students apply the truths learned through the story of the Shunammite and her son. First, review the Bible story. Then have students work their way through the maze (without peeking at the memory verse!) by following each letter of the word. Warning: Some of the letters don't belong!

What to Say

When the kind woman of Shunem was helpful to the prophet Elisha, she received help too. When her son was brought back to life, she discovered an amazing fact about God: He can be trusted to help. That's a discovery you can make every day!

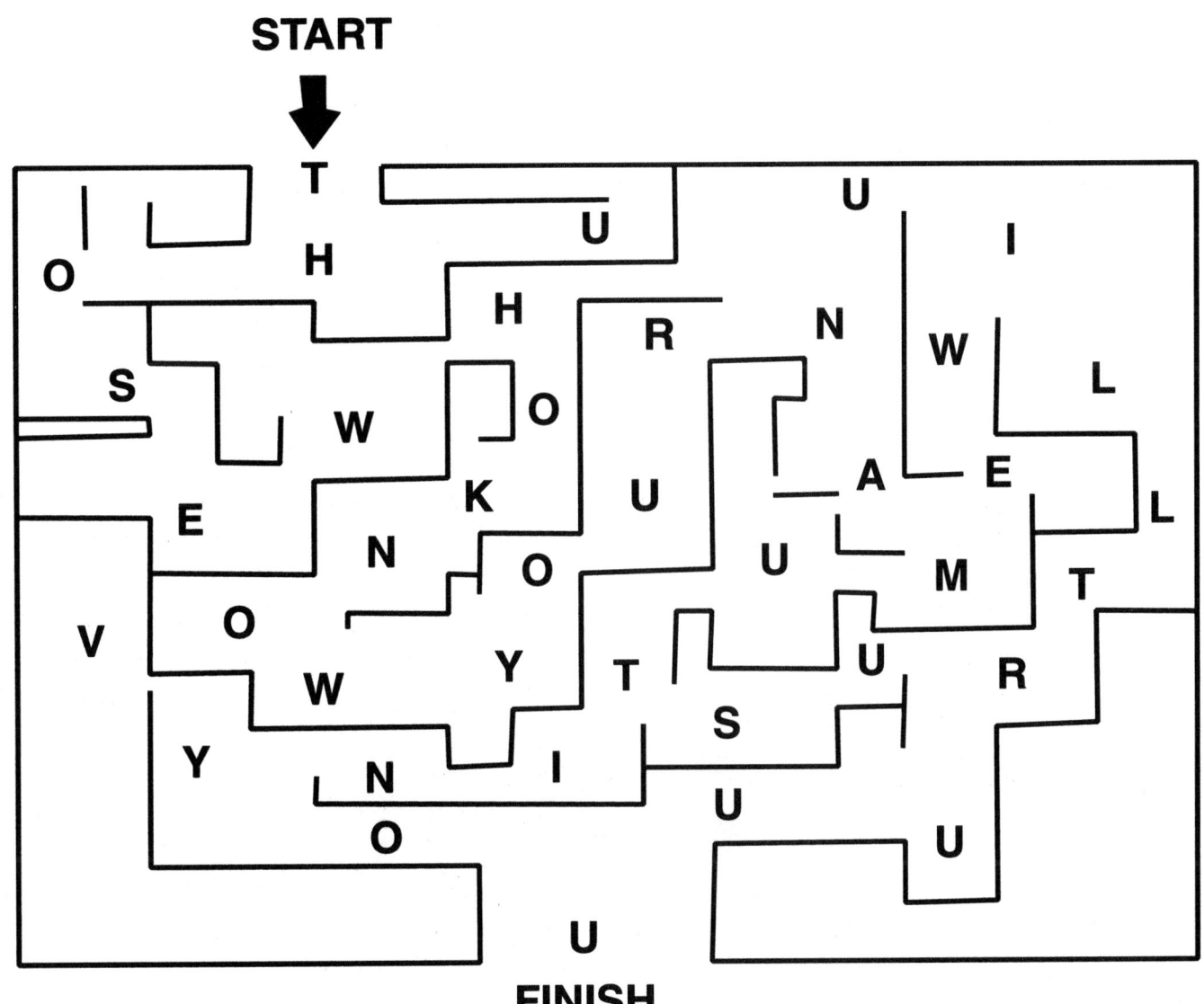

START

FINISH

Naaman's Servant Girl

Serving the Master
❧ 2 Kings 5:1-16 ❧

Memory Verse

Love your enemies, do good to them, and lend to them without expecting to get anything back.
~Luke 6:35

What You Need

• pan of water
• towels
• masking tape
• four buckets with handles

What to Do

To help students learn about the duties of Bible-time servants, use the following activities. Explain that a servant usually washed the feet of his or her master's guests as a sign of hospitality (refer to John 13:1-17, when Jesus washed His disciples' feet). Let the students take turns washing each others' feet or hands. Then explain that another job of servants was to fetch and carry. Try this relay (you might want to play outside): Divide the students into two teams. Line each team single file at one end of the room. Make a masking tape finish line on the opposite side of the room. Put water in four buckets (about half-full). Give two buckets to the first person in each team. When you say, "Go" each person should race-walk to the finish line and then back to tag the next teammate. The first team to finish wins.

What to Say

Bible-time servants had difficult lives. Sometimes they served cruel masters. Many times they had been forced into slavery after being captured by enemies. Naaman's servant girl had been forced into slavery after being taken from her country. She was fortunate to be in a household where her master treated her fairly. Some slaves had the responsibility of taking their masters' children to school and minding them. All servants were expected to obey their masters. Slaves had to carry water, cook meals or do whatever was expected of them.

Naaman's Servant Girl

A Difficult Kindness
✑ 2 Kings 5:1-16 ✑

Memory Verse

Love your enemies, do good to them, and lend to them without expecting to get anything back.
~Luke 6:35

What You Need

• page 48

What to Do

Duplicate page 48 for each student. Have a girl student read the servant girl's part as the narrator. Select a boy student to read the other speaking parts. Instruct the girl to pause when the boy speaks. Afterward, have a time of prayer, allowing the students to pray for a willingness to do good even to those who mistreat them.

What to Say

How did the servant girl show kindness to her master? Do you think she expected anything in return? Why or why not? Naaman's servant girl could have been angry. After all, she had been captured from her country and forced into slavery. How would you have felt? Yet she willingly helped her master when he needed help. Her example reminds us to treat everyone with respect. Would you have treated your master with kindness? How do you act when people mistreat you?

Help for a Master

I work for a man named Naaman. Naaman is the commander of the army of Aram. Being a slave isn't always easy. But at least my master and mistress treat me kindly.

I felt sorry for my master because he had leprosy. That's a horrible skin disease. People suffer a lot with leprosy. I knew that if my master went to the prophet Elisha, he would be healed.

I told my mistress, "If only my master would contact the prophet in Samaria."

My master listened to my advice. He went to the king of his country asking for permission to go. The king sent a letter to the king of Israel. The king of Israel was scared.

"Am I God?" he asked. "Why would this other king send someone to me to be cured of leprosy? Maybe he is trying to pick a fight."

Somehow the prophet Elisha heard about Naaman and the note. He sent a message to the king of Israel and told him to send my master to his house. So that's where my master went.

But he did not see the prophet. Elisha sent a messenger to tell my master what to do.

"Go and wash in the Jordan River seven times," Elisha told him. "Then you will be healed."

My master is a proud man. He did not want to wash in the Jordan River. He asked if he could wash in rivers he liked better.

But some of my fellow servants were with my master. They told him that obeying the prophet was good. So he did. And guess what? He was healed!

I'm glad I was able to help my master.

Joash

Memory Verse

God is our refuge and strength, an ever-present help in trouble.

~Psalm 46:1

What You Need

• page 50
• pencils

What to Do

Duplicate page 50 for each student. Explain that there were two boy kings of Israel, Joash and Josiah (see page 52). Let the students read Joash's story in 2 Kings 11. You can have students take turns reading the whole chapter or just the following verses: 1-5, 8, 12-15 and 19-20. Afterward, instruct the students to put the events of Joash's "road" to the kingship of Israel in order.

Introduction

Can you imagine being president of the United States at your age or even younger? Joash and Josiah both became kings of Judah before they were nine years old! Being king is a big responsibility. But they had help from relatives and other important people in their lives. Joash had to face some real trouble before he became king. Thankfully, he could count on God to help him. What big tasks are you responsible for? Who are the people who help you with those tasks? How do they help? How has God helped you recently? Sometimes God helps us by giving us caring people to help us.

The Road to the Kingdom

Joash had a hard road to take before becoming king. Put these events of his life in order. Number the footprints 1, 2, 3 and so on.

____ Jehosheba hides Joash in the temple.

____ Athaliah decides to get rid of the princes in line for the throne.

____ Jehoiada crowns Joash as the king of Judah.

____ Joash, age 7, takes the throne.

____ Joash, just a year old, lives with his nurse in the temple while Athaliah rules the land.

____ Athaliah hears the people cheering.

____ The people cheer for Joash.

____ Jehoiada declares that Athaliah be put to death.

____ Jehoiada the priest shows Joash to the guards. He makes them promise to guard him.

Josiah

Doing Right for God
2 Kings 22:1-11, 18-20

Memory Verse

He [God] guides the humble in what is right and teaches them his way.
~Psalm 25:9

What You Need

• duplicated page
• pens
• crayons

What to Do

Photocopy this page for each student. Have the students take turns reading Josiah's story in 2 Kings 22:1-11. Explain that many sports players have cards that tell all about them. Review the Josiah card with them then ask the students to think about a card for themselves. Encourage them to consider the important information they would want people to know about them, then use the blank card to fill in those things.

What to Say

The Bible tells about many of Israel and Judah's kings. Some of these kings were good. Others were bad kings. Josiah was only eight years old when he became king of Judah. His own father, like his father before him, did bad things. But Josiah "did what was right in the eyes of the Lord" (2 Kings 22:2). Later in his life, he found the book of the Law in the temple. The book of the Law was one way God guided Josiah to do what was right. One way God guides us is through His Word, like Josiah found. One thing the Bible tells us is "Do not follow the crowd in doing wrong" (Exodus 23:2). When are you tempted to follow the crowd? How can you do "what is right in the eyes of the Lord" like Josiah?

**Followed God.
Had the temple repaired.
Found the book of the Law
and wanted to obey God.**

Joash and Josiah

Setting an Example
♪ 2 Kings 11; 22:1-11, 18-20 ♫

Memory Verse

Don't let anyone look down on you because you are young, but set an example for the believers in speech, in life, in love, in faith and in purity.

~1 Timothy 4:12

What You Need

- poster board
- markers
- pencils
- construction paper
- scissors

What to Do

Give each pair of students a poster board. Have the students read the memory verse together. Explain that Paul wrote these words to Timothy, a young man who was a pastor. Instruct the students to make a memory verse poster, showing a way kids can "set an example for the believers in speech, in life, in love, in faith and in purity" as 1 Timothy 4:12 advises. They can copy the verse on their posters. Suggest that they make their posters lively and three-dimensional. Decorate your classroom with the posters.

What to Say

Many people who are role models think about setting a good example for others. Joash and Josiah set an example of following God. If you think that just because you're a kid you can't set an example, think again!

naming Babies

Bible-Times names
∽ Isaiah 7:14; 8:1-10; 9:6-7 ∾

Memory Verse

And he will be called Wonderful Counselor, Mighty God, Everlasting Father, Prince of Peace.
~Isaiah 9:6

What You need

• page 54
• pencils

What to Do

Duplicate page 54 for each student. They should use the code to finish the statement. Explain that Isaiah was an Old Testament prophet. The answer is on page 96.

What to Say

Names meant a lot to the Israelites. Whenever God suggested a name to a parent-to-be, He had a point to make. When the prophet Isaiah had a son, God wanted the baby's name to show that trouble would come to Israel. The name Maher-Shal-Hash-Baz meant that another country would carry off Israel's possessions. But there would come another baby hundreds of years later whose name would be a sign of hope.

Signs of the Times

God had a sign of hope for Israel. A special baby would be born with a special name. Use the code at the bottom of the page to finish the statements below based on Isaiah 7:14 and to answer the question.

A young, unmarried woman will have a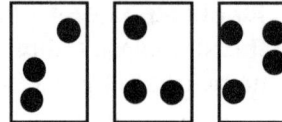

and will call him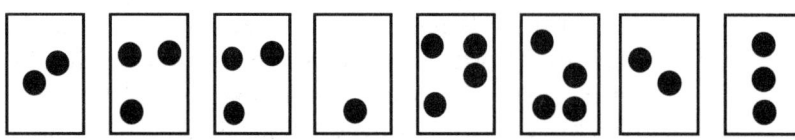

___ ___ ___

___ ___ ___ ___ ___ ___ ___ ___

which means

"___ ___ ___ with us."

Who is this special child?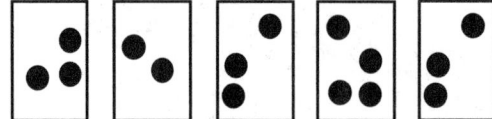

___ ___ ___ ___ ___

A   D   E   G   H   I   J   L   M

N   O   S   T   U   W

54

Naming Babies

Memory Verse

And he will be called Wonderful Counselor, Mighty God, Everlasting Father, Prince of Peace.
~Isaiah 9:6

What You Need

- poster board
- markers

What to Do

Read the memory verse together. Give each pair of students a poster board and have them make memory verse posters celebrating the many names for Jesus. Let the kids draw pictures showing what all or some of these names mean to them. For example, for "Everlasting Father," they might show a father with a child.

What to Say

The prophet Isaiah predicted Jesus' birth hundreds of years before Jesus was born. Jesus was the promised Messiah, the Savior of the world. Jesus has a lot of names. As a "Wonderful Counselor" Jesus gives wise advice. Being "Mighty God" means that Jesus is no mere man. He is God. Being an "Everlasting Father" means He is eternal. Being the "Prince of Peace" means that He brings us peace. All of the these names add up to one thing: He is God.

John the Baptist

The Gift of a Son
✍ Luke 1:5-25, 57-80 ✍

Memory Verse

Thanks be to God for his indescribable gift!
~2 Corinthians 9:15

What You Need

• pages 56 and 57

What to Do

Duplicate this page and page 57 for each child. The story of John the Baptist's birth is a fun story to sign. Work through each of the four signs below (some of which were used on page 33) with the students, repeating them until everyone is comfortable with the actions. Have readers take turns reading the narration as everyone signs.

What to Say

Imagine getting a gift you never thought you would — something you always wanted. That's how Zechariah and Elizabeth felt. They always wanted a son. But they could not have children. So Zechariah prayed to God. God showed in an amazing way that He had heard Zechariah's prayer.

God

Point index finger (the sign for G) forward, then bring whole hand backward and down.

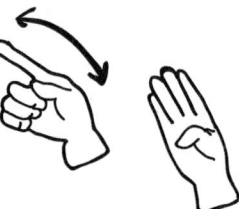

Children

Place right hand in front of body, palm facing down. Move hand up and down as if patting someone shorter on the head.

Son

Move hand against forehead, then place hand in crook of arm.

Speak (Say)

Use the right index finger to make a small, circular movement in front of mouth.

The Gift of a Son

There once lived a priest named Zechariah. He was married to a woman named Elizabeth. They both served God (*use sign for God*). But they could not have children (*use sign for children*).

One day while Zechariah burned incense in the temple, an angel suddenly appeared to him. Zechariah drew back in fear.

The angel said, "Do not be afraid. I have come to tell you that your prayers have been heard. Your wife, Elizabeth, will have a son (*use sign for son*). You are to name him John. He will be a joy to many people. He is never to drink wine. He will be filled with the Holy Spirit from the day of his birth. He will make the people ready for the Lord."

Zechariah was surprised. "How can I know this is true? I'm old and so is my wife."

"I am Gabriel," the angel said. "Daily, I stand in the presence of the Lord (*use sign for God*). I have been sent to tell you this good news. Because you did not believe me, you will not be able to speak (*use the sign for speak*) until all that I said happens."

And so Zechariah could not speak (*use sign for speak*) a word.

Finally, Elizabeth gave birth to a son (*use sign for son*). Eight days later, when it was time to name the baby (*use sign for son*), Elizabeth was asked what his name would be. The people thought he would be named Zechariah, after his father.

Elizabeth said, "The child (*use sign for son*) is to be called John."

"But there is no one in your family named John," one of the people said.

The people used signs to speak (*use sign for speak*) to Zechariah, asking him what to call the baby (*use sign for son*).

Zechariah wrote on a tablet, "His name is John."

Suddenly, he could speak (*use sign for speak*)! Zechariah praised God (*use the sign for God*). Everyone was amazed and gave God (*use the sign for God*) praise.

John the Baptist

John's Special Vow
♫ Luke 1:5-25, 57-80 ♫

Memory Verse

We…will give our attention to prayer.
~Acts 6:3-4

What You Need

• page 59
• pens

What to Do

Duplicate page 59 for each student. Give each child a copy as you discuss the importance of daily prayer. Encourage your students to use this page as a way to plan a special time to meet with God each day for at least a week. Show how they can list their prayer requests and their answers to prayer.

What to Say

The angel Gabriel told John the Baptist's parents that their son was special. He would be a Nazirite. That meant he would not drink wine. He would be filled with the Holy Spirit from birth. This special vow meant that John would be serious about serving God. After all, his mission was to prepare the hearts of the people for the Savior! How serious are you about serving God? One way you can be serious is to build up a prayer habit. How? Make a point of being in prayer every day.

Sunday

Time I'll meet with God: _____

Prayer Requests:

Answers:

Monday

Time I'll meet with God: _____

Prayer Requests:

Answers:

Tuesday

Time I'll meet with God: _____

Prayer Requests:

Answers:

Wednesday

Time I'll meet with God: _____

Prayer Requests:

Answers:

Thursday

Time I'll meet with God: _____

Prayer Requests:

Answers:

Friday

Time I'll meet with God: _____

Prayer Requests:

Answers:

Saturday

Time I'll meet with God: _____

Prayer Requests:

Answers:

John the Baptist

John's Arrival
Luke 1:5-25, 57-80

Memory Verse

Children [are] a reward from him.
~Psalm 127:3

What You Need

• duplicated page
• pencils

What to Do

Have the students read the memory verse together to reinforce the concept. Then explain that the pinball machine will "work" when the story pictures of John the Baptist's birth are in order. They should write a number in the box by each picture (there is one picture that shows something that did not happen — they should put an X across that one). For each one they get right, they can award themselves the amount of points by each picture. If they correctly cross out the "phony photo," they get 50 points for that too.

What to Say

Having a child is always a blessing. A child was a special blessing for Zechariah and Elizabeth, who were unable to have children for a long time.

60

Jesus

Memory Verse

For nothing is impossible with God.

~Luke 1:37

What You Need

• duplicated page

What to Do

Copy this page for each student. Ask if the students can recall when Gabriel had a major part in another Bible story. (He came to Zechariah with news that Zechariah and his wife Elizabeth would have a son.) Have the students act out the story below using the script. The student playing Mary should be seated. Explain that the Bible does not say for certain what Mary was doing when the angel came to see her.

What to Say

What is the longest you have ever waited for something? When you're waiting, even a minute can seem like an hour. Can you imagine waiting 700 years for something? Not likely! The coming of the Savior — the Messiah — had been foretold 700 years before Jesus was born. That moment was nearly at hand. A young woman named Mary is just about to get an important announcement — one that will change her life completely. Mary was little more than a teenager at this point in her life. How would you have felt if you were Mary?

Narrator: God sent the angel Gabriel to Nazareth to visit a young woman named Mary. Mary was engaged to be married to a carpenter named Joseph.

Gabriel: Greetings! You are favored of God.

Narrator: Mary wasn't sure what that greeting meant.

Gabriel: Don't be afraid, Mary. You will give birth to a child. You are to call Him Jesus. He will be great. He will be called the Son of the Most High.

Mary: How can this be? I'm not married.

Gabriel: The Holy Spirit will come upon you. The one to be born will be called the Son of God. Even Elizabeth, your relative, is to have a baby in her old age. And she could not have children. Nothing is impossible with God.

Mary: I am the Lord's servant. May everything be done as you said.

Narrator: So the angel left Mary.

Jesus

A Savior Is Born
✏ Luke 2:1-20 ✏

Memory Verse

Today in the town of David a Savior has been born to you; he is Christ the Lord.

~Luke 2:11

What You Need

• duplicated page

What to Do

Use the story below with the inserted songs to open or close your class during the Christmas season (or have Christmas in July!) Explain that "Messiah" means "Christ" or "the anointed one."

What to Say

Jesus was the Savior that had been promised to the people long ago. Instead of being born in a palace like any other king, He was born in a stable. Although the story of Jesus' birth is a familiar one, the wonder of that night long ago still lives on.

Caesar, the Roman emperor, made a law that everyone in the land was to be taxed. So Mary and Joseph had to travel all the way from Nazareth to Bethlehem. There, they would be counted with those of David's family line.

Mary was almost ready to have her baby. So the long journey was not easy.

When they reached Bethlehem, they found no place to stay. They had to stay in a stable. There Mary gave birth to a son and laid him in a manger.
(**Sing** *"Silent Night" and "Away in the Manger."*)

There were shepherds in the area watching over sheep at night. Suddenly, an angel appeared to them. They were very afraid!

"Do not be afraid," the angel said. "I have good news for you. Today, a Savior has been born to you in the town of David. He is Christ the Lord. You will find Him wrapped in clothes and lying in a manger."
(**Sing** *"Hark the Herald Angels Sing."*)

Before the shepherds could move, a whole army of angels appeared in the sky. They all cried out, "Glory to God in the highest. On earth, peace, good will toward men."(**Sing** *"It Came Upon a Midnight Clear."*)

The angels left just as quickly as they had appeared. "We must see what has happened," the shepherds said. They wasted no time in running to Bethlehem.

They soon found Mary, Joseph and the baby. Just as the angels said, the baby lay in a manger. They were amazed! The Messiah had been born! They gave thanks to God.
(**Sing** *"Joy to the World."*)

Jesus

Jesus Is Here!
♪ Luke 2:1-20 ♪

Memory Verse

Today in the town of David a Savior has been born to you; he is Christ the Lord.

~Luke 2:11

What You Need

• page 64
• scissors
• construction paper or cardboard
• acrylic gloss
• varnish
• yarn
• string
• glue
• paintbrushes
• glitter, buttons or beads

What to Do

Duplicate page 64 for each student. They can select one of the patterns to make a stringed Christmas ornament. After they cut out the pattern, have them trace around it on cardboard or construction paper. Help the students apply the gloss and varnish to the construction paper. Make sure they coat the entire surface. Before the varnish dries, have them add string or yarn in a design on the pattern (use cotton or yarn to give the sheep "wool"). They should brush more varnish over the string. They can also add glitter or other decorations.

What to Say

We celebrate the coming of Jesus at Christmas time. Knowing that God kept His promise to send a Savior makes us feel joyful. We put up decorations to share our joy with others. How many of you have a favorite Christmas ornament? Why is it your favorite? What will you tell others about the meaning of this ornament?

Jesus

Memory Verse

Ascribe to the Lord the glory due his name; worship the Lord in the splendor of his holiness.

~Psalm 29:2

What You Need

• pages 65 and 66

What to Do

Duplicate this page and page 66 for each student. Have them take turns reading the story below, then show how to use the code to complete the story.

What to Say

What is the most expensive gift you've ever received? Jesus received some expensive gifts — the kinds of gifts kings usually received. He did not receive these gifts from family members. He received them from people who traveled many, many miles just to catch a glimpse of Him. These wise men from the East didn't follow a road map to get to Jesus. They followed a star.

When Jesus was born, Herod was the king of Judea. Some wise men called Magi came from the East to find this newborn king. They stopped in Jerusalem to ask Herod about the child.

"Where is the newborn king of the Jews?" they asked. "We saw His star in the East. We have come to worship Him."

King Herod did not like this news. He called the chief priests together to ask them where Jesus had been born. "In Bethlehem," they told him. They repeated the Old Testament prophecy about the Messiah's birth.

Herod called the Magi. "Go to Bethlehem. When you find the child, let me know. I want to worship Him, too."

But Herod did not want to worship the child. He was lying.

As the magi went on their way, they saw the star again. They were filled with joy. They soon found the house where Mary, Joseph and the child lived. They worshipped the child, then presented Him with gifts.

What gifts did the Magi bring? (Use the code to figure out the gifts. Check Matthew 2:11 also.)

The Magi were warned in a dream not to go back to Herod.

The Magi gave Jesus:

__ __ __ __

      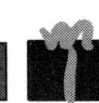

__ __ __ __ __ __ __ __ __ __ __ __

__ __ __ __ __

What would you give Jesus? _____

Jesus

Escape to Egypt
✎ Matthew 2:13-23 ✎

Memory Verse

Even though I walk through the valley of the shadow of death, I will fear no evil, for you are with me.

~Psalm 23:4

What You Need

• duplicated page
• pencils
• Bible dictionary

What to Do

Duplicate this page for each child. Have the children look up facts about Herod in a Bible dictionary and discuss them. Explain that the Romans were really in charge of the land. Then distribute the mazes for the children to complete.

What to Say

Herod, the ruler of Judea, was jealous of Jesus, the newborn king. Herod did not want anyone to take away his power. After the Magi refused to tell Herod where the child was, Herod gave orders to kill all boys two years old and younger. But God protected the newborn king. An angel appeared to Joseph in a dream to take Mary and Jesus to Egypt. A while later God let Joseph know it was safe to leave Egypt. They left to make their home in Nazareth. Even though fearful things happen to us, we don't have to be afraid. God is always with us.

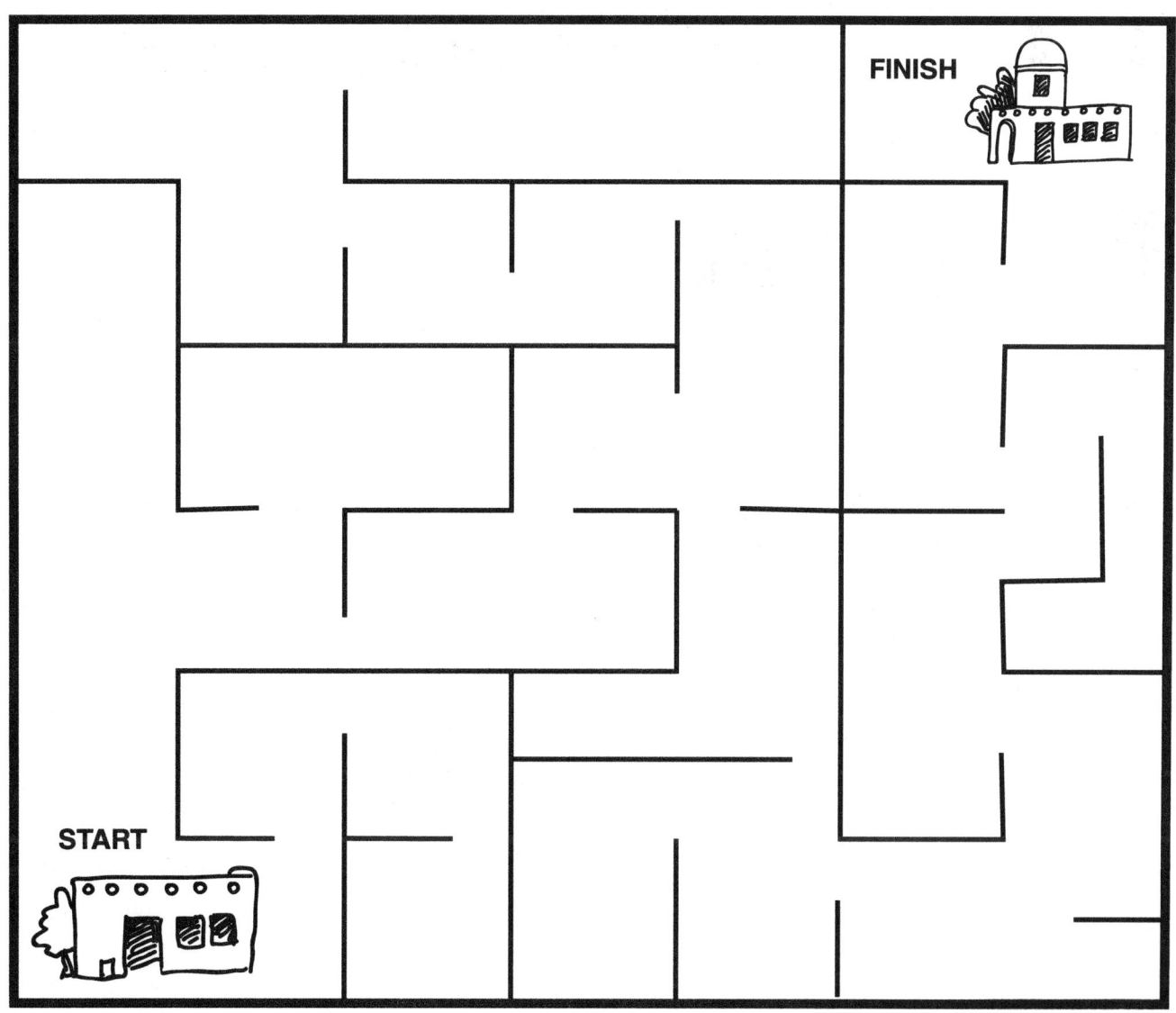

Jesus

Memory Verse

A good name is more desirable than great riches; to be esteemed is better than silver or gold.
~Proverbs 22:1

What You Need

• baby name book
• felt or poster board
• scissors
• glue
• construction paper
• markers

What to Do

Most name books include the meaning of each name. During class, look up your students' names in the book and what each name means. If you cannot find some names, look up the child's middle name or the root of that name (i.e., Anne=Anna; Glynnis=Glenn). If a name still cannot be found, assign that child a characteristic based on his or her God-given gifts and talents. Explain that Jesus' name means "the Lord saves." Encourage the children to use the supplies above to make a name banner for themselves.

What to Say

The Jewish people had a tradition. Male babies were to be named on the eighth day. Names were important. When Jesus was eight days old, Mary and Joseph presented Him at the temple. On that day, they named Him Jesus, just as the angel told Mary to do. Jesus certainly lived up to His name! He did exactly what His name means. Some names do not provide us with a mission like Jesus' did. But God still calls us Christians. That's a name we can all live up to. How will you live up to yours?

Jesus

A Good Son
Luke 2:41-52

Memory Verse

Children, obey your parents in the Lord, for this is right.

~Ephesians 6:1

What You Need

• pages 70-72
• pencils

What to Do

Before class, duplicate page 70 for each child. Copy the signs from pages 71-72. Tape the signs on opposite walls. Explain to the students that the caravan traveling to Jerusalem had to travel nearly 100 miles and that at the age of 12, boys prepared to take their place in the community, which would be official when they turned 13. Have one student read the story. The rest of the students can be part of the traveling caravan. Have Jesus and the caravan travel back and forth from "Nazareth" to "Jerusalem." After the students perform the story, have them answer the questions that follow.

What to Say

Although it's hard to believe sometimes, Jesus was once a kid, too. Like you, He had to listen to His parents. But He also had a heavenly Father to whom He was to listen.

A Son Is Missing

Jesus and His family went to Jerusalem every year. Traveling from Nazareth to Jerusalem took three whole days. The roads were also dangerous, because robbers were around. So people traveled in big groups. Mary and Joseph went to Jerusalem to celebrate Passover and other special holidays.

The group was headed back to Nazareth when Joseph and Mary made a terrible discovery.

Jesus was missing! He was not with the other children in the group. He wasn't anywhere!

Mary and Joseph searched everywhere! Finally they knew there was only one place He could be.

Jerusalem.

Three days later, they found Him in the temple. There He talked to the temple leaders. He asked them hard questions. They were amazed that a 12-year-old could ask such questions.

"Son, how could You worry us like this?" Mary asked.

"Why did you look for Me?" Jesus asked. "Didn't you know I had to be in my Father's house?"

Mary and Joseph did not understand what He meant.

Jesus went home with them and was obedient. He grew in wisdom and in God's favor.

Why was Mary worried?

_____

Where was Jesus? What was He doing?

_____

How do your parents show their concern for you?

_____

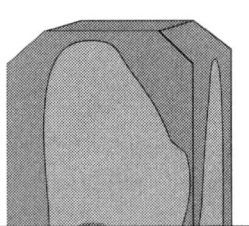
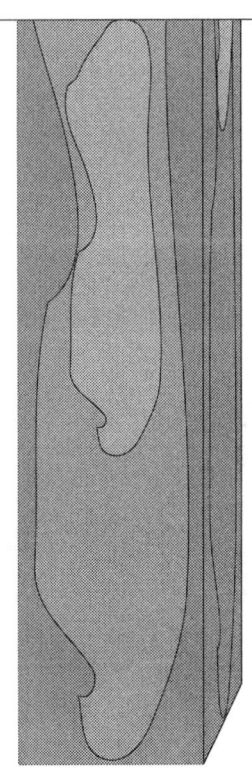

TO NAZARETH

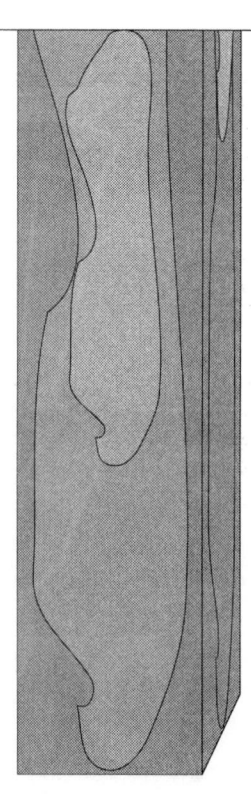

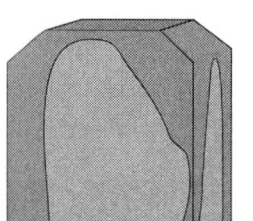

TO
JERUSALEM

Jesus

One Amazing Life
Matthew 2; Luke 1:26-56; 2

Memory Verse

I have come that they may have life, and have it to the full.

~John 10:10

What You Need

- page 74
- bulletin board
- construction paper
- markers
- instant camera

What to Do

Copy page 74 for each child. Label your bulletin board "Jesus and Me" by using stencil letters or write with a marker on poster paper. Ask a student to print the memory verse on construction paper, using different colored markers. Snap a photo of each student with an instant camera. Mount a collage of the photos on the bulletin board. Distribute the copied sheets and ask the students to write about how Jesus' coming changed their lives. Add the sheets to the display. Attach a rendering of Jesus to the board. In the coming weeks, continue to take pictures to mount on the bulletin board as examples of how Jesus came to give life "to the full" as John 10:10 states.

What to Say

Prophets like Isaiah gave the Israelites hope about the coming Messiah. People during Old Testament times looked forward to the birth of the Savior hundreds of years before it happened. Finally the Savior arrived! Jesus' coming changed the world. Nothing would be the same! Think about how Jesus' coming changed your life. What would you like to tell others about how Jesus changed your life?

How Jesus' coming changed my life

_____

_____

_____

_____

_____

_____

_____

_____

name: _____

Jesus

A Son to Come
∽ Genesis 3:1-7, 15 ∾

Memory Verse

For the wages of sin is death, but the gift of God is eternal life in Christ Jesus our Lord.

~Romans 6:23

What You Need

• page 76
• scissors
• glue

What to Do

Duplicate page 76 for each student. Have the students cut out the puzzle pieces and glue them onto the circle. Once your students put the puzzle together, read the verse together.

What to Say

Adam and Eve's sin caused all of us to become separated from God. But God promised to send someone special to make things right. Only this person could bring people back to God. The promise in Genesis 3:15 means that God would send a Savior someday.

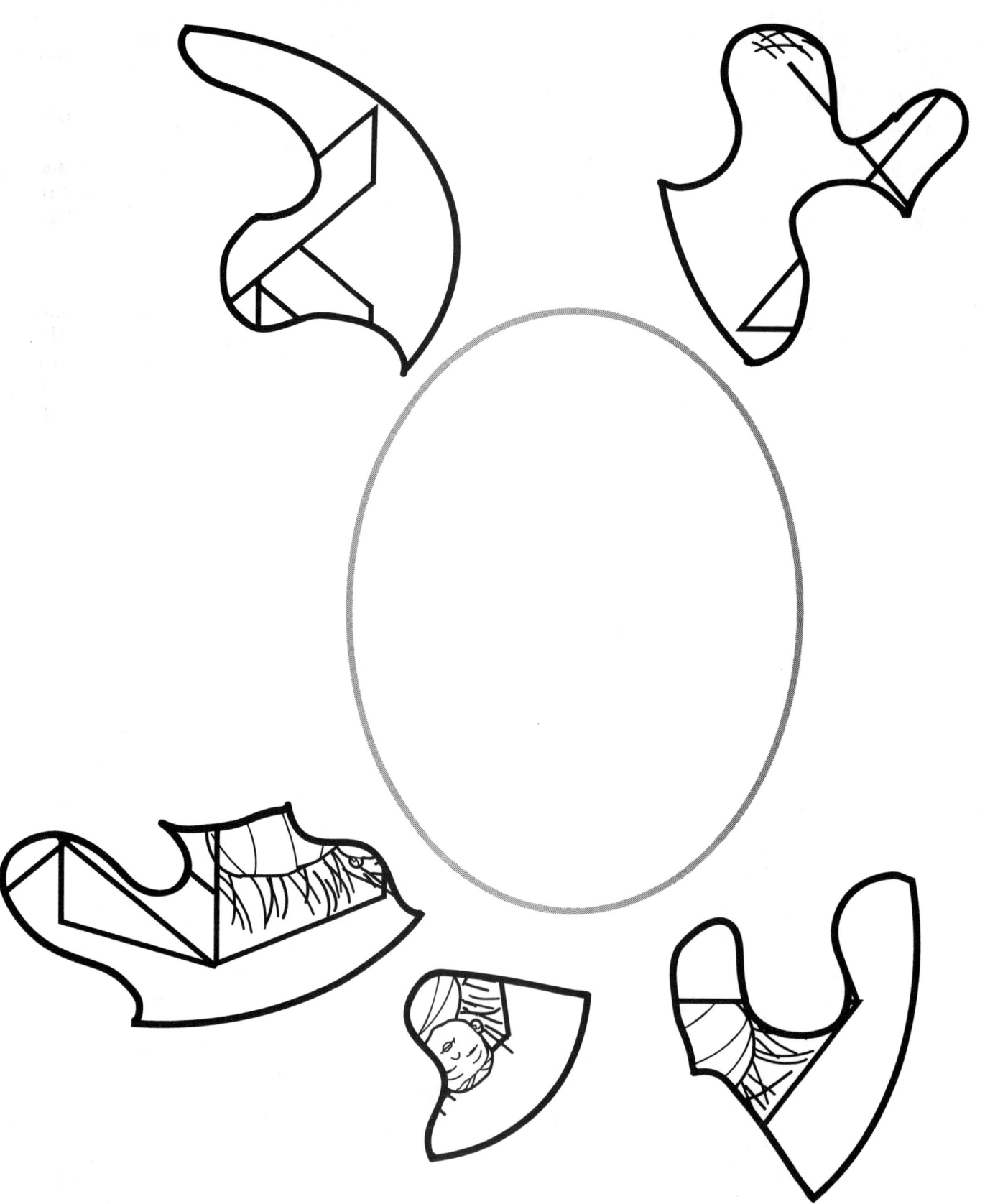

The Boy Who Gave His Lunch

Lunch for 5,000
John 6:1-13

Memory Verse

Give, and it will be given to you.
~Luke 6:38

What You Need

• page 78
• chairs
• construction paper
• marker

What to Do

Make two copies of page 78. Set up your class area as a television studio with two chairs, a construction paper sign labeled "Amazing Stories" and chairs for your "audience" (the students). Select two students to play the host and the "Lunch Boy." Give them each a copy of the script to perform. (See page 80 for a dip recipe to make while the story is performed.)

What to Say

Jesus met and helped a lot of children. One child in the Bible wanted to help Him! We don't know his name; we just know what he did. He was willing to share his lunch with others. But with over 5,000 people to feed, a miracle-working Savior was needed. What this boy gave was given back to him, as the memory verse says. Can you think of something you gave that was given back to you?

Amazing Stories

Host: Hello, and welcome to Amazing Stories. I'm your host, Barry Cling (Terri Cling, if played by a female.) We're here talking with…talking with…Excuse me, what did you say your name was?

Lunch Boy: I didn't. Just call me Lunch Boy. Everyone does.

Host: Unusual name.

Lunch Boy: That's not my real name. When people think of me, they think of how I once gave my lunch to Jesus.

Host: Tell us about it.

Lunch Boy: I was in the crowd that followed Jesus up on a mountainside. People talked about how He had healed the sick. We wanted to see Him do something amazing.

Host: And did He?

Lunch Boy: Yes!

Host: What? Tell us? The public demands to know.

Lunch Boy: I would tell you if you would stop interrupting. My father says it is not polite to interrupt. (Pauses briefly to see if the Host will interrupt, then go on.) Anyway, I heard Jesus ask Philip.

Host: Tell us who Philip is.

Lunch Boy: One of Jesus' disciples. Like I was saying before I was interrupted, Jesus asked Philip, "Where can we buy bread for all of these people?"

Host: How many people were there?

Lunch Boy: Over 5,000!

Host: Wow! I would suggest a lot of pastrami! And maybe a nice tossed salad.

Lunch Boy (glaring at Host): You're doing it again.

Host: Sorry!

Lunch Boy: Philip told Jesus, "Even eight months' wages won't buy enough bread for this crowd." That's when I realized I had food to share. I gave my lunch to Andrew.

Host: Who is Andrew?

Lunch Boy: Another of Jesus' disciples. He's Peter's brother.

Host: So what happened after that?

Lunch Boy: I'm getting to that. Andrew told Jesus, "This boy has five barley loaves and two small fish. But how will that be enough to feed everyone?"

Host: Yes. What were you thinking?

Lunch Boy: It doesn't matter what I was thinking. What matters is what Jesus did. He told the disciples to have everyone sit down in groups. After giving thanks, He started handing out food. He kept giving out bread and fish until everyone had enough to eat! Isn't that amazing?

Host: That's my line. As host of Amazing Stories, I'm supposed to say that.

Lunch Boy (ignoring Host): Jesus told the disciples to gather up the leftover food. They filled 12 baskets! I'll never forget being with Jesus that day. I'm sure glad I shared my lunch.

Host: That's it for this week's edition of Amazing Stories! Tune in again next time!

The Boy Who Gave His Lunch

Bread to Eat
☙ John 6:1-13 ❧

Memory Verse

Therefore I tell you, do not worry about your life, what you will eat or drink.
~Matthew 6:25

What You Need

• page 80
• see ingredient list on page 80

What to Do

What better way to talk about the story of how a boy shared his lunch than by eating? Copy page 80 for each child as a take-home sheet. Gather supplies to make the dip below. Have pita bread or Hawaiian bread available to dip. Explain that the boy probably had small, round barley loaves and sardine-like fish. Many poor people could only afford barley loaves. If you have an adventurous group of children, bring a can of sardines to class and let them sample!

What to Say

When a small boy shared his lunch, thousands had plenty to eat — with help from Jesus, of course. Jesus taught His disciples a lesson that day. They learned that with God they did not have to worry about what they would eat.

Bread and Dip

Make a tasty dip to serve on bread.
- 1 package of Hidden Valley Ranch Dressing™ (dry mix)
- 1 cup of shredded cheddar cheese
- 1/4 cup of bacon bits
- 1 (one) 16 oz. cream cheese (softened)
- mixing spoon
- mixing bowl
- hand mixer (optional)

Soften the cream cheese. If you use pre-whipped cream cheese, you will not need the hand mixer. Slowly add the cheese, bacon bits and ranch dressing mix to the cream cheese, stirring each time. Now your dip is ready!

Therefore I tell you, do not worry about your life, what you will eat or drink.
Matthew 6:25

Jairus' Daughter

Through the Crowd
✎ Matthew 9:18-19, 23-25 ❧

Memory Verse

Everything is possible for him who believes.
~Mark 9:23

What You Need

• two brooms
• several blocks
• chairs
• seeds, marbles or blocks
• bandannas or scarves
• sandbox shovels

What to Do

See the instructions below for two games that will help you explain the story of Jairus' daughter.

What to Say

Although we don't know the name of Jairus' daughter, we do know that Jesus touched her life in a special way. This young girl was dead — a problem beyond human ability. But her father, Jairus, had the foresight to seek the God of impossibilities.

Games

To prepare your students for the story of how Jesus helped Jairus' daughter, choose from one of the following icebreaker games:

Game 1: Set up three to four chairs in two areas a few feet apart from each other vertically, but not in a straight line. Divide your kids into two teams. Give a broom to the first child in each team. Place a pile of blocks at his or her feet. He or she is to sweep the pile from one end of the room, around the chairs, and back to tag the other teammates. The first team to have all of its members sweep the pile through the chairs can be first for snack time. Or, provide prizes for all the children. Use the game to talk about how Jesus was "swept" through the crowd by Jairus, who needed Jesus' help for his daughter.

Game 2: Scatter seeds or blocks in piles on the floor or table. Divide your students into pairs. Blindfold one person in each pair with a bandanna or scarf. Give the "blind" people a shovel. Have them try to pick up the scattered items with their partners' guidance. The sighted partner should not touch any of the scattered material. He or she is only to give vocal instruction. After the blocks are picked up, scatter them again and let the blind partners become the guides. After the game, explain that picking up the scattered items would be nearly impossible without help. Then explain that Jairus needed Jesus' help in an impossible situation.

Jairus' Daughter

An Impossible Task
ஃ Matthew 9:18-19, 23-25 ஃ

Memory Verse

Everything is possible for him who believes.
~Mark 9:23

What You Need

• page 83

What to Do

Copy page 83 and give each child one. Have the students act out the TV news show. Explain that although there were no TV shows during Bible times, the facts described in the script are real. If your group is particularly inventive, have them write and perform their own drama, based on the Scripture.

What to Say

A man named Jairus came to Jesus with a problem: his daughter was sick. Jesus was willing to help this sad father. But before they arrived at Jairus' home, they received bad news: his daughter was dead! It was too late for Jesus to help. Or…was it?

Amazing Stories (Jairus' Daughter)

Cast

Host
Jairus
Jairus' daughter

Host: Hello, and welcome to Amazing Stories. I'm your host Barry Cling (Terri Cling, if played by a female). Our guests tonight are Jairus, a synagogue ruler, and his daughter.

Jairus: Glad to be here.

Jairus' daughter (looks frightened): Hello.

Host: Jairus, tell us in your own words what happened to you.

Jairus: Actually, nothing happened to me, except I met the most wonderful person in the world: Jesus. My daughter's the one you should be talking to.

Host (to Jairus' daughter): How old are you?

Jairus' daughter: Twelve.

Host: Tell us what happened. (There is a brief silence. Host turns to Jairus.) Not much of a talker is she?

Jairus: She's still thinking about what Jesus did for her. It was amazing!

Host: That's why we wanted to have you both on Amazing Stories. Tell us, what's so amazing about your story?

Jairus: My daughter was dead and now she's alive!

Host: Really?

Jairus: Yes! You see, my daughter was very sick. I was very worried about her. I'd heard about Jesus, and about the wonderful miracles He had performed. Some had been saying that He was the Messiah. I had to find Him. So I walked straight up to Him and...

Jairus' daughter: Father, you're forgetting about the crowd. There were so many people surrounding Jesus. You could barely get through to talk to Him.

Jairus: You're right. That's exactly what happened.

Host (to Jairus' daughter): So what happened next?
(There is a brief silence. Host turns to Jairus.) So, what happened next?

Jairus: I asked Jesus to come to my house. The two of us walked to my house.

Jairus' daughter: Father, three of Jesus' disciples went with you, also. Peter, James and John.

Host (to Jairus' daughter): Did your father know you were dead at this time?
(There is a brief silence.) Is it me, or does your daughter just dislike talking?

Jairus: She's a little shy talking in front of so many people. Anyway, when we were on our way, some of the men from my house came to us and said, "Don't bother the Teacher. Your daughter is dead." When we arrived at the house, everyone was crying in mourning. Jesus said, "Why are you all crying? The girl is not dead. She's just asleep." Isn't that so? (He looks at daughter. She nods.) The mourners laughed at Him.

Jairus' daughter: You told me Jesus made them all leave.

Jairus: That's true. We went in where my daughter was lying. Jesus took her by the hand and said some words in Aramaic, which mean, "Little girl, get up!" And she did!

Host: Amazing! What a story! Well, that's all the time we have, folks. Join us again next time when we'll bring you another edition of Amazing Stories.

Jairus' daughter: Wait! I didn't get to talk!

Host: Next time, dear.

Jairus' Daughter

Healing a Daughter
℘ Matthew 9:18-19, 23-25 ℘

Memory Verse

Everything is possible for him who believes.
~Mark 9:23

What You Need

• page 85
• pencils

What to Do

Duplicate page 85, give each child a copy and allow them to complete the maze. Then have a time of prayer for the "impossible" situations in your students' lives. Many eight- and nine-year-olds think most of the problems of their lives are impossible, so do not correct them if they ask for prayer for a situation that is easily solved. If the problem distresses them, it's time to take it to God!

What to Say

When a child is sick, parents do whatever they can to help him or her. But some problems are beyond a parent's ability to solve. That is when parents bring in the experts — people who know what to do. That is just what Jairus did. He went to the expert problem-solver. Jesus can solve impossible problems that no one else can.

START

FINISH

Jairus' Daughter

Help for the Hard Times
Matthew 9:18-19, 23-25

Memory Verse

Never will I leave you;
never will I forsake you.
~Hebrews 13:6

What You Need

• pages 87 and 88
• heavy paper
• crayons

What to Do

Copy page 87 on heavy paper and page 88 on regular paper for each child. Show how to cut out both pieces and cut the slits in the plain piece. Allow them to color the pieces. Demonstrate how to thread the illustrated sheet through the slits, so one phrase and picture shows, then another.

What to Say

Jesus helped Jairus through a difficult time in his life. We go through hard times in our lives sometimes, too. But God promises to be with us always. Give this slider reminder to a friend or family member who is going through a difficult time.

JESUS CAN TURN OUR SADNESS

INTO JOY!

Blessing the Children

Coming to Jesus
ஃ Matthew 19:13-15 ஃ

Memory Verse

Jesus said, "Let the little children come to me...for the kingdom of heaven belongs to such as these."

~Matthew 19:14

What You Need

- page 90
- heavy paper
- markers
- scissors
- glue
- glitter
- construction paper

What to Do

Copy page 90 on heavy paper for each child. Have them cut out the hanger and the insert. They can draw a picture of Jesus welcoming children or Jesus welcoming them. They should write their names on the blank line. Allow the children to use markers, construction paper and glitter to decorate the hanger. If there are children in your class who do not know Jesus as Savior, be sure to answer any questions they may have.

What to Say

Jesus gathered children near Him to bless them and pray for them. He prays for you, too. He also gave us the Holy Spirit as a sign that He is always near. The descending dove on your doorknob hanger is a sign of the Holy Spirit coming down. Use the doorknob hanger as a reminder that Jesus invites you to come to Him.

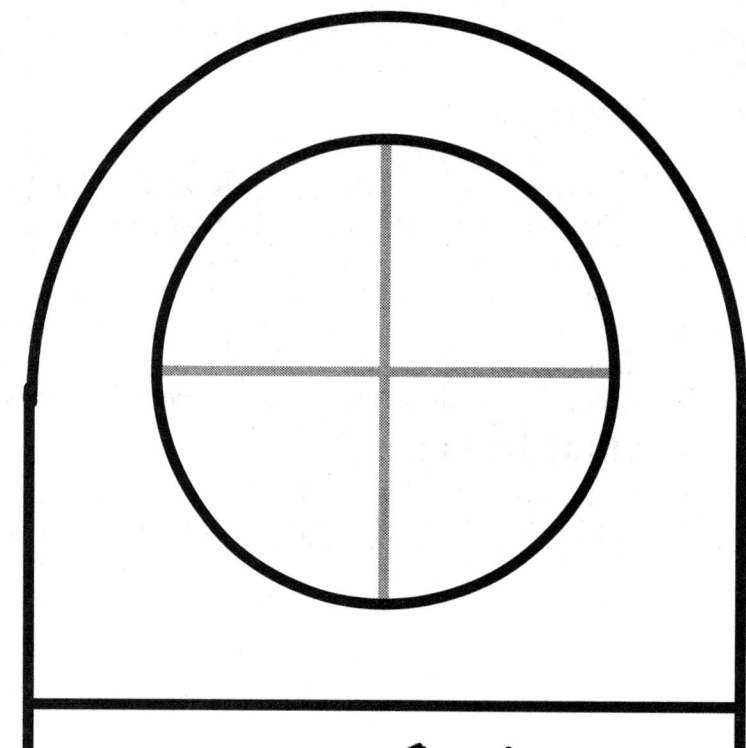

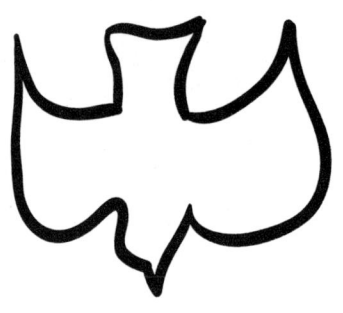

Jesus said, "Let

_____

come to me."
(Based on Matthew 19:14)

Blessing the Children

Jesus Welcomes the Children
ᔏ Matthew 19:13-15 ᔐ

Memory Verse

Jesus said, "Let the little children come to me...for the kingdom of heaven belongs to such as these."

~Matthew 19:14

What You Need

• no materials needed

What to Do

Act as the storyteller by reading the poem below. Divide the group in half. Half can act as the disciples while the other half are the children to be welcomed. The activity is even more effective if an adult dressed as Jesus comes to say His lines and perform His actions. The "disciples" can say "No, go away," after you read the speaker tag. The disciples should shake their fingers at the "children" and try to chase them away from Jesus. After you read the poem, have your students think of ways they can welcome others like Jesus.

What to Say

Jesus was never one to turn anyone away. He welcomed all types of people. One day a special group of people came near to be blessed. The disciples weren't happy to see them. But Jesus taught the disciples an important lesson — no one is to be turned away from Him.

A Poem to Perform

(*As the poem is read, perform the actions.*)

Jesus invited the children all to come.
(*Have children make a welcoming gesture by waving their hands toward them.*)
The disciples said, "No, go away."
(*Have children wave hands away from them.*)
They did not want the children, not even some,
To bother Jesus that day.

But Jesus said, "Let the children come near.
(*Have children make a welcoming gesture by waving their hands toward them.*)
Don't hold back anyone."
The kingdom belongs to these who are here."
Then He placed His hands on each one.
(*Have children go around the room and briefly place a hand on each others' heads as a sign of blessing.*)

Blessing the Children

All Are Welcome
Matthew 19:13-15

Memory Verse

Jesus said, "Let the little children come to me...for the kingdom of heaven belongs to such as these."

~Matthew 19:14

What You Need

- page 93
- dowel rods
- scissors
- hole punch
- markers
- fishing line

What to Do

Duplicate page 93 for each student. Have them cut out each figure. They may draw themselves and their friends or family on the people figures or they can write their names on each one. Show how to punch a hole in each figure at the black dot. Have the children cut several lengths of fishing line. Show how to pull an end of the line through the hole in each figure and make a knot. Demonstrate how to hang each figure from the dowel, starting in the center. Also tie a length of line in the center to hang the mobile.

What to Say

Jesus blessed the children who came near Him. Even today, He never pushes anyone away. He wants everyone to come to Him. That includes you! Use this mobile as a reminder that Jesus invites you to draw near to Him. When you look at the mobile, pray for each person who you drew or whose name you wrote.

Answer Key

page 17

Ninety-nine
Eighty-nine
Children
Angels
Son
Laugh

page 18

page 27

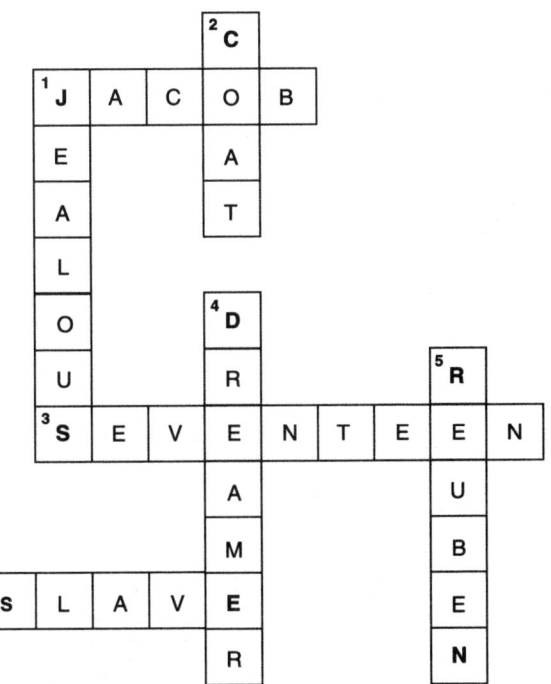

page 30

page 35

nine
servants
Eliab
boasting
stones

page 40

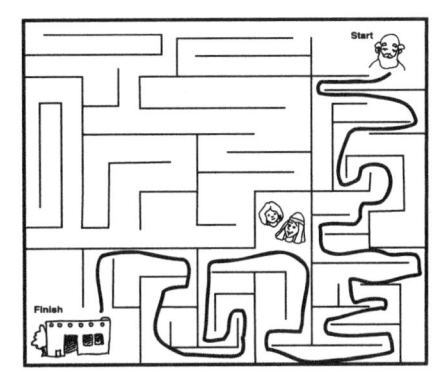

page 44

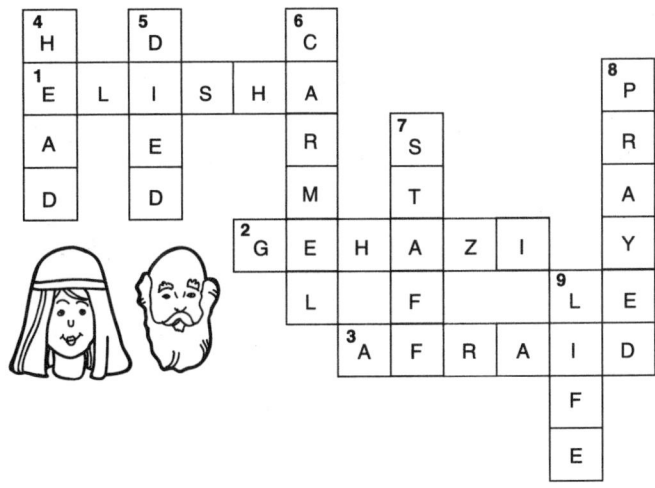

page 45

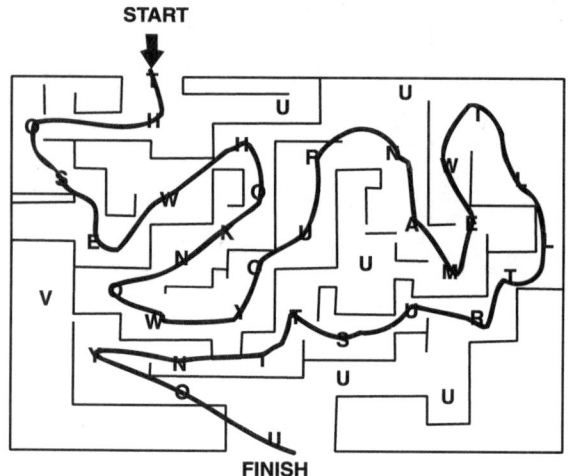

page 66

gold
frankincense
myrrh

page 67

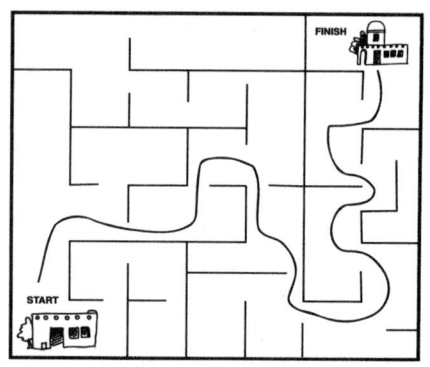

page 50

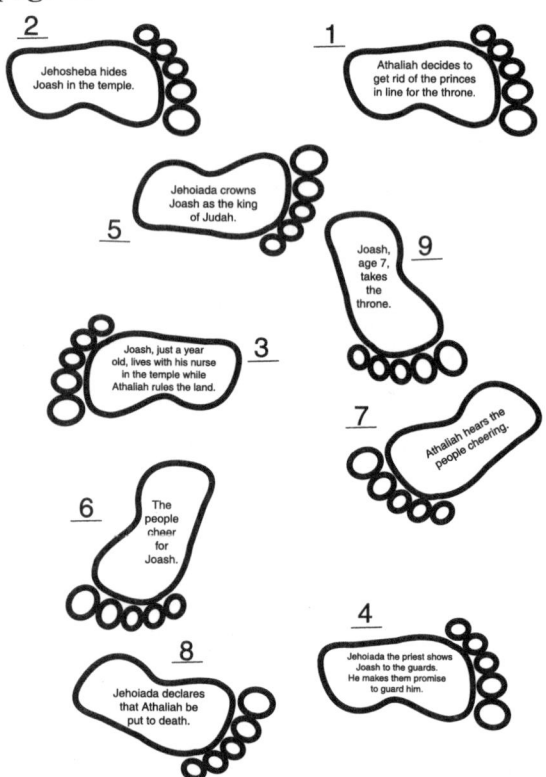

page 76

page 54

son
Immanuel
God
Jesus

page 85

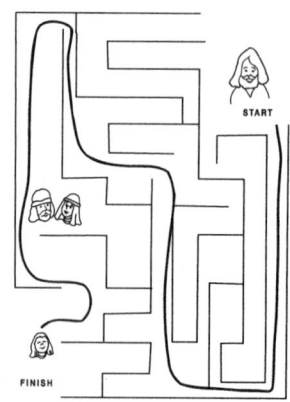

page 60